ALSO BY OLIVER NIÑO

Spiritual Activator: 5 Steps to Clearing, Unblocking, and
Protecting Your Energy to Attract More Love, Joy, and Purpose

The above is available at your local bookstore,
or may be ordered by visiting:

Hay House USA: www.hayhouse.com®
Hay House Australia: www.hayhouse.com.au
Hay House UK: www.hayhouse.co.uk
Hay House India: www.hayhouse.co.in

***

DO THIS BEFORE BED

SIMPLE 5-MINUTE PRACTICES
THAT WILL CHANGE YOUR LIFE

OLIVER NIÑO

HAY HOUSE LLC
Carlsbad, California • New York City
London • Sydney • New Delhi

Published in the United States by:
Hay House LLC, www.hayhouse.com®
P.O. Box 5100, Carlsbad, CA, 92018-5100

Project editor: Melody Guy • *Cover design:* 99designs
Interior design: Karim J. Garcia • *Interior photos/illustrations:* Shutterstock

**Cataloging-in-Publication Data
is on file at the Library of Congress**

Hardcover ISBN: 978-1-4019-8003-0
E-book ISBN: 978-1-4019-8004-7
Audiobook ISBN: 978-1-4019-8005-4

11 10 9 8 7 6 5 4 3 2
1st edition, March 2025

Printed in the United States of America

This product uses responsibly sourced papers, including recycled materials and materials from other controlled sources.

The authorized representative in the EU for product safety and compliance is Penguin Random House Ireland, Morrison Chambers, 32 Nassau Street, Dublin D02 YH68, Ireland. https://eu-contact.penguin.ie

CONTENTS

INTRODUCTION

How do you typically wake up in the morning? Are you refreshed, well rested, and eager to start the day? Or are you more likely to hit the snooze button on your alarm multiple times before dragging yourself out of bed for a strong cup of coffee? Do you feel you have all that you need to be present and engaged for both yourself and your loved ones? Or do you find yourself frantically running through a to-do list that kept you awake with stress the night before?

If you're like most people, you might often wake up feeling out of sorts and disconnected from your natural state of joy and ease. But what if you could change the way you wake up by changing how you go to sleep? What if you could transform how you experience your day, and even your life, by tapping into the power of something every single one of us already does: falling asleep at night?

Do This Before Bed: Simple 5-Minute Practices That Will Change Your Life is packed with tips and techniques I've developed from 20 years of supporting clients and students across the globe. I wrote this book to offer you a sustainable way to a better life by shifting your mindset and reprogramming your subconscious mind through simple, effective practices you can do at bedtime.

All of us want to live our best life, but so often, that goal can feel distant—even improbable. But it isn't. Living a life of wholeness, in which all our deepest needs and desires are easily and rapidly met, is our birthright. And that's exactly what this book will help you achieve, every day and every night.

Why Bedtime?

One of the questions I often hear from students and clients is, "Why is it so important to do these practices before bed?" While it may be tempting to zone out over Netflix, especially at the end of a long workday, the period of time right before we shut our eyes is crucial when it comes to the quality of our waking hours.

Our bedtime routines can help us to connect with our mind, emotions, and energy—elements often neglected during the day because our attention is taken up by other matters such as work, relationships, family, and finances. However, whatever we focus on before we go to bed deeply influences how we experience our waking hours.

Thankfully, the science of sleep has evolved to deepen our understanding that bedtime is a potent tool for our well-being. Sleep scientists have noted that the habits we practice at bedtime can enable not only deeper sleep but also greater cognitive, physical, mental, and emotional health. Establishing a sleep routine that helps us drift off with greater ease and relaxation regulates the circadian rhythm, the internal clock that oversees functions such as digestion, body temperature, energy fluctuations, and our sleep-wake schedule. In addition, it releases something known as homeostatic sleep pressure, which is caused by a chemical called adenosine; as we stay awake, adenosine builds up in our brains and gives us the physical response of sleepiness. Good sleep literally purges adenosine and helps us wake up feeling bright-eyed and bushy-tailed, exuberant and refreshed.

During sleep the mind sifts through all the information it received during the course of the day, simultaneously working to regulate our emotions and physical functions, and manage the giant warehouse of memories within the brain. So, the time before sleep is important because it determines not just the quality of our sleep but also the mindset we take into our waking hours. And beyond that, sleep also opens us up to our fertile subconscious mind, which we access through dreams and deep-sleep states.

The subconscious mind stores all the information that's connected to anything and everything we've ever experienced. In fact, most of who we are exists outside our conscious awareness. The conscious mind, also known as the ego, is responsible for analyzing, making decisions, problem-solving, fixating on specific memories, and forming and clinging to opinions. In contrast, the subconscious mind holds a broader range of information that gets filtered through the conscious mind, which would be way too overwhelmed by the sheer volume of details.

The subconscious mind harbors the key to more expansive states because it contains possibilities that live beyond our limited perceptions of reality. Scientists have suggested that approximately 5 percent of our brain functions are conscious and deliberate, and 95 percent are subconscious and automatic. This is why working with the subconscious, which we'll be doing *a lot* of in this book, is so powerful; it's where we can start to unlock more of our potential.

The subconscious mind is always working in the background, and the period of time leading into sleep is especially powerful when it comes to programming it. The French psychologist Émile Coué was well aware of this and encouraged depressed patients to repeat, "Every day in every way I am getting better and better," several times before falling asleep.* Coué called this the power of *optimistic autosuggestion*, which is basically positive reinforcement. It worked, and there are documented letters from several of his patients who reported major improvements in their physical and mental

---

* Émile Coué. *Self-Mastery through Conscious Autosuggestion*. Republished from the author's original manual. G&D Media: 2019.

health—including overcoming depression, chronic pain, and insomnia. Some of them genuinely believed the statement, while others were less convinced but nevertheless still experienced positive results. Coué's work demonstrates that our conscious beliefs don't necessarily matter; it's when the subconscious mind has absorbed the belief that we start experiencing it as if it were reality.

How does this work? Many mindfulness practitioners, hypnotherapists, and sleep scientists now theorize that the period before falling asleep marks a natural hypnotic state during which brain waves slow down and the mind is ripe for reconditioning. In this state, we can plant new ideas that bypass our usually loud and opinionated conscious mind that wants to immediately rear its head and say, "Well, that's not very realistic, is it?" With that normally overbearing voice safely on its way to sleepy town, the subconscious mind can readily receive and absorb new messages and ideas—such as our vision of perfect health, or our intent to make better decisions—as if they are real . . . and then, they *will* be.

This might sound like magical thinking, but it isn't! It's an automatic tendency known as confirmation bias, where we seek support for our preexisting beliefs and ignore any information that conflicts with those beliefs. You might think you're conscious of all your beliefs, but the deepest ones exist at the level of your subconscious mind. So, when you program the subconscious mind with new, more vibrant, more expansive beliefs (which this book will help you to do), you will attract conditions in your external reality that are a match for those beliefs.

Overall, the practices in this book are designed to bypass the limiting messages we hold in our conscious awake state about what we're capable of. Instead, they help us embed high-intensity, positive ways of being, thinking, and acting

DO THIS BEFORE BED

in our subconscious and create a new matrix for reality as we know it. From this place, we can literally make magic.

Inventor Thomas Edison famously stated, "Never go to sleep without a request to your subconscious." Additionally, self-help entrepreneur Napoleon Hill said, "Your subconscious mind works continuously, while you are awake and while you sleep."

Throughout this book, you'll be making a lot of requests to your subconscious mind, and the benefits will multiply. You'll bring yourself into a state of calm and open receptivity. You'll de-stress and experience better sleep. You'll wake up with more energy. You'll free yourself from anxiety-inducing thoughts that interfere with your sleep and waking hours. You'll also feel more connected to your higher self, that part of you that is so much bigger than your conscious mind and life circumstances, so that you feel a greater sense of connection with yourself, your loved ones, the world, and the divine (or whatever higher power you believe in). You'll prime your subconscious mind to help you create what you desire most.

Who Am I? And Why This Book?

I've been called a lot of things in my adult life: an energy healer, spiritual activator, lightworker, influencer . . . but the truth is, I'm a normal guy whose out-of-this-world spiritual awakening led me to my soul's mission: rescuing humans from suffering, as quickly as possible, and helping them experience their truest, most empowering potential.

Like many of the people who walk through the doors of my energy healing school, I faced a significant amount of adversity early in life. I was bullied as a child and never felt like I fit in. In many ways, I didn't feel like I related to kids my age. I tended to prefer deep conversations with older people, like family members and my father's colleagues. I spent a lot of time alone at school, so I was pretty low in the pecking order—with no friend group or social circle to speak of—making me an easy target. Over time, school became a painful place to be, and I spent most of my days trying to remain invisible. Fortunately, I had creative outlets that helped me a lot: I wrote songs and played guitar, and as a teen, I was in a few bands and made friends outside of school.

However, what little stability I found with my creative pursuits was shattered when my parents faced the prospect of bankruptcy. My mother came from a wealthy family, so I grew up with a great deal of privilege in an environment where all my needs were taken care of. My father was an ambitious entrepreneur who launched several businesses. However, his venture into the rice industry nearly led to bankruptcy, causing my father to downsize. Overleveraged with loans and debt, he couldn't pivot or fix it fast enough. After the business went belly-up, we moved from one of the best neighborhoods in town to one of the worst. I went from having it all to having the rug pulled from under my feet. All this created a major conflict in my identity, and a great deal of shame. Continuing to go to an exclusive private school made me feel like an impostor. I didn't want anyone to see or know the real me.

The chaos was compounded by my internal suffering . . . by this nagging feeling that I was inadequate and imperfect compared to my peers and family members, and that I'd never be good enough. This was my version of normal, and these feelings persisted throughout young adulthood.

Then, when I was 18, my parents moved our entire family from the Philippines to the U.S. Again, whatever stability I'd managed to find disappeared in an instant. This was an especially rough patch, particularly because things were going relatively well for me at the time. I had a girlfriend, a band, and

DO THIS BEFORE BED

a new college life, and I was being forced to leave my friends and culture behind. I had to start over—a stranger in a strange land. For the first three to six months after we moved to the U.S., I spiraled into a depression that felt like it would never end. I barely wanted to leave my room. I watched everyone from my past seemingly move on without me. It was one of the most isolating periods of my life, but ironically, it birthed my passion for personal development. I poured my life into reading self-help and psychology books, and signed up for programs that would give me insight into the inner workings of the mind. I was proactive when it came to learning skills that would allow me to improve my relationships with myself and others. It was a defining moment. Once I hit the cold, hard earth of rock bottom, there was nowhere to go but up.

In fact, this has been a recurring theme in my life: starting from scratch . . . and building up from nothing. However, as much as I was learning and progressing, I still noticed myself repeating a lot of the same patterns that had characterized my early life: I'd build a business or undertake an exciting new venture. I might even enjoy success for a while, but then, something would happen to upset it all—maybe the business would go bankrupt or I'd find some other way to self-sabotage.

Over time, I started to see that I was stuck in a looping pattern. My history was becoming my future. Toxic relationships followed me everywhere, and I was deeply unhappy, no matter how much money or abundance I had. Years before I realized that empathy was one of my superpowers, I was already deeply sensitive to other people's energy. As a result, I was a people pleaser who always tried to sense what others wanted and needed, and constantly put myself last.

After spending a few years throwing money at my problems to make them go away, I realized that my efforts were futile. Money couldn't solve this issue—I needed to do deeper work. I noticed that some methods worked better for me than others, and among those, only a few worked consistently. Throughout this exploratory process, I recognized the power and importance of collecting tools that would work for me, regardless of my circumstances—and even my beliefs!

What I quickly came to see is that, no matter what you think or how you feel—and no matter your age, race/ethnicity, background, or level of trauma—there are certain principles and techniques that universally work for everyone. These tools would change my life for the better. I now run a eight-figure business alongside my wife, Mandy. We have three beautiful children, gorgeous homes across the country, and have created a community of heart-centered souls (two million strong and growing!) from all walks of life who are constantly regaling us with their success stories.

And that's ultimately what this book is about—giving you the methods that will help you write your own success story!

I've spent the better part of two decades performing energy healings and reaching millions of souls whom I've taught to detox their energy so they can create the life they desire—one that's always in alignment with the universe's highest good. In my certification program, Geo Love Healing, I help individuals master their energy, unblock themselves from mental, emotional, and energetic obstacles, and become certified healers and life coaches. I lead workshops, spearhead events, and teach online and in-person sessions to students from all over the world. They experience results *fast*, and I strive to be authentic and supportive during their journeys, as I share everything I've learned (mostly self-taught), which I see as one of my most important responsibilities and purposes in this lifetime.

I've performed more than 20,000 healings and trained close to two million students online, from over 60 countries.

I receive literally thousands of e-mails each month from souls who share their success stories with me. This is how I know the tools and techniques in this book work. And if you stick with them long enough, they'll work for you too.

The Greek philosopher Socrates knew that the ultimate form of freedom and self-mastery was to "know thyself." I believe this wholeheartedly. Once we know ourselves well enough, and we have the confidence that comes from being equipped with the tools to navigate any situation, regardless of how intense it is, we can meet our lives with the kind of courage and openness that generates miracles.

If you're sitting there thinking, *Oh no, not another guy telling me he has the magic solution to all my problems*, I totally understand. And I'm not here to ask you to believe—I'm here to ask you to commit to implementing the tools in this book.

Also, please know that your past is not your future! Even if you've been through debilitating ups and downs, you can actively create the life of your dreams right here and now. All it takes is a few minutes before bedtime. You don't need to believe in any of the New Age woo-woo stuff—heck, you don't need to believe in anything at all! All I ask is that you be, in the words of one of my students (a self-professed skeptic), at least 5 percent open to the teachings in this book. Soon enough, you'll be using them to help yourself and others step into a life of greater abundance, peace, joy, purpose, and freedom.

The Structure of This Book and How to Use It

The practices in this book are designed to help you develop basic bedtime routines that engage your mind, emotions, and energy to help you achieve what you want at an accelerated pace. While this might sound outlandish, there is a deeply practical and scientific foundation to these methods, which is explored in Chapter 2. Through these practices, I offer an array of tools—visualization, intention-setting, breathwork, crystal therapy, movement, journaling, and so much more—that I've witnessed create major identity shifts and miracle after miracle in the lives of ordinary people who go on to do extraordinary things.

To that end, *Do This Before Bed* is meant to be your personal bible for healing and wholeness in all aspects of your life. It's not meant to remain on a shelf, never to be opened. I hope you'll keep it by your bedside—dog-ear it, write notes in it, share it with friends and family, and come back to it over and over.

Do This Before Bed is organized around two pillars. The first consists of foundational practices, which you'll learn in Part 1. These are four bedtime practices that will optimize your life and increase your sense of well-being and vitality. The remaining chapters in Part 2 comprise the second pillar: practices to heal and manifest the life of your dreams.

You may choose to use *Do This Before Bed* in a nonlinear way, as a practical resource you can draw upon for a specific need or phase of life (e.g., becoming a parent, ending a long career, etc.), but I encourage you to read through the entire book and become comfortable using the foundational practices in Part 1 for at least a month before diving into the other tools. Over time, you should be able to move through all four foundational practices in five to ten minutes—however, I encourage you to err on the side of taking more time with them, especially at first, and doing them as often as you can throughout the day. That way, you'll build the stamina to layer in additional practices that might be a little more time-consuming, similar to how we build strength over time when we get into an exercise routine.

Part 2 is divided into 17 chapters on a range of topics, from love to abundance to creativity. You'll find two to three practices at the end of each, as well as my insights about each topic, which I hope will offer meaningful context for how you can start to reframe existing preconceptions. All the chapters include personal stories and case studies from students and clients who worked with the practices and achieved significant results. I kept the chapters brief and to the point, because I don't want you to get bogged down in theory. I want you to practice!

These practices are designed so that the larger consciousness that facilitates your capacity to magnetize what you want and need is activated, even as you sleep. Many of the practices in this book focus on setting a powerful intention, which is essentially the same as sending a prayer out into the universe. Often, when you hear stories of people praying for something and miraculously receiving what they prayed for, it isn't necessarily because they believed in the power of prayer. It's the act of setting an intention (prayer) that drops you out of your logical mind and into your heart, which is the gateway to the soul— and the heart also happens to hold the largest electromagnetic field in the body.

So, no matter what you believe or even whether you believe, the practices in this book will move you into the optimal frequency to achieve your heart's desires. Even though you're using your mind to read the instructions I offer, the mind isn't the most powerful player in this game—nor is it the part of you that will be the most engaged in the process. *Do This Before Bed* enables a much more effective system—the divine patterns we're each born with, which are independent of the mind—to kick in. For example, you don't have to believe you were born with a heart in order for it to beat; it beats without your conscious effort, because it is part of the inherent pattern with which you came into this world.

Do This Before Bed isn't centered around one particular goal or one particular reader. I've worked with everyone from stay-at-home moms building six-figure businesses in the healing arts, to Olympic medalists looking to optimize their performance (and their joy), to world leaders grappling with some of the most complex problems imaginable, to curious students of life who are eager to discover their purpose or make the right decision for themselves at a major turning point. What they all have in common is that they're looking to improve their life in every domain.

Our modern existence can be stressful, and while it's not always possible to immediately change our external circumstances, we can change our internal mindset. In the words of Dr. Wayne Dyer, "If you change the way you look at things, the things you look at change."

The clarity and accessibility of these practices will help you frame the journey toward your best life as a set of rituals that are as easy and mundane as, say, brushing your teeth, eating three meals a day, or getting a physical checkup. They will quickly become second nature, and the prospect of "inner work" will never feel like hard work again. *Do This Before Bed* is about helping you recognize that life can be so much easier than we tend to make it. We know the shortest, quickest way to get what you want is by moving in a straight line, from point A to point B. Instead, we take all kinds of roundabout routes to get to where we want to go, based on rules and conditions that don't hold up under close scrutiny. When we follow those rules and conditions, we're only prolonging the inevitable: our return to our natural birthright, which is a state of happiness, wholeness, and the realization that we can transform our life for the better . . . sometimes, in mere moments.

I encourage you to keep a journal close to your bed so that you can chart all your hopes, thoughts, wishes, and dreams (some of them nighttime dreams!), and also make any notes about your progress. It may be subtle at first, but keeping an ongoing record will allow you to see just how much you've changed. My hope is that *Do This Before Bed* will lead you into the most mind- and heart-shifting transformations of your life. May you discover even more abundance, joy, and purpose than you ever dreamed possible.

PART 1

FOUNDATIONAL PRACTICES FOR OPTIMAL ENERGY HYGIENE

All the practices in this book, particularly the four foundational ones you'll be learning shortly, are focused on energy hygiene. This involves simple but powerful tools to cleanse lingering, unwanted energy to ensure that your physical body, energetic body, and emotions are free of external and internal influences that make it hard to focus on living your best life.

Often, the traditions we grow up with already incorporate some form of energy hygiene. My student Carla shared that she was forced to say prayers at bedtime every night by her religious parents. Although she was initially resentful of this nightly routine, which strictly prescribed an obedience to a God she barely knew if she believed in, she came to appreciate it as she got older. Gradually, the rote and predictable requests she made to this invisible divinity turned into personal reflections and intentions that matched her heart's desires.

Carla says, "Over time, prayer became a refuge for me. I didn't necessarily ask God for things all the time; instead, prayer became a way for me to get the events of the day off my chest and clarify for myself the kind of life I wanted. Prayer was literally an opportunity for me to dream the life I wanted into existence."

Although prayer wasn't necessarily something she initially chose to end her day with, it has become an important foundation for all the inner work she's done and has accelerated every aspect of her life in ways I hope you'll soon become intimately familiar.

More than four decades later, Carla still says her prayers at bedtime, but she has now added the four foundational practices you'll soon learn about. They comprise the core basic practices for achieving a sense of greater clarity, purpose, and possibility each day. If you do only these four practices and nothing else in this book, I'll consider my work well done. Of course, I hope they're just the start of this journey for you, but I'm confident that incorporating them into your bedtime routine will change your life. Hopefully you will find these four foundational practices so fun and appealing that you'll do them every single night to infuse your life with joy and positivity. Having used them over many decades, I've learned to tailor my routine, doing all four when necessary or just one or two as needed.

When I started doing the foundational practices, I was distracted and all over the place, preoccupied with all the stuff on my to-do list and how I could accomplish the most in the least amount of time. This interfered with my sleep, causing me to recognize that something had to change. I began researching the power of planting seeds in the subconscious mind right before going to sleep. The changes I experienced were almost instantaneous. Within a week, my sleep issues dissipated. I felt calmer and more present, capable of responding from my deepest values rather than reactivity or habit.

I slowly started introducing these practices in my work as a way of helping my students and clients shift their energy. Invariably, they experienced similar results as they discovered that they were so much bigger than their conscious mind and its limitations. Their success stories are too numerous to count.

One client, Gary, who'd never held down a meaningful or well-paying job for more than six months at a time, launched a six-figure business within three months. Another client, Dina, who had been in a string of toxic relationships that had contributed to addiction and suicidal ideation, built up the courage to leave her abusive marriage once and for all, and to become a fierce advocate for other people in similar situations. Gary, Dina, and so many of my other clients and students were also doing a lot of tangible work in their day-time hours to contribute to these huge transformations, but they've attributed their relative ease and success to the time they dedicated to their bedtime routines—or, as my student Carla now puts it, "my holy meditation-prayer-magic time." I'm sure that as you build the practices into your life, you'll experience the same thing.

CHAPTER 1

THE 411 ON ENERGY WORK

Throughout history, different cultures and traditions have recognized a universal life force that flows through our bodies and minds. You can call it prana, chi, pneuma, or simply your breath—it doesn't really matter. Whatever your preferred label, this energy encompasses our intuitive awareness (helping us pick up on good or bad vibes before our brain has had adequate time to process information), our physical state, and our mystical potential. It is the life force that flows through all aspects of who we are, especially the ones we cannot see. Energy, the very source of our power, can be experienced as abundance or depletion, affecting our access to power. And while we still don't have a fundamental answer as to what exactly energy is, we have demonstrable evidence that it exists—and that it can be neither created nor destroyed, but only transformed.

When we're talking about "energy medicine," lots of people think of that as a vague or woo-woo concept—less a measurement of something "real," like calories or watts, and more of a metaphor. However, energy medicine is very much real, and there have been plenty of people in the fields of psychology and the hard sciences who've begun to build a sophisticated, non-esoteric understanding of how it works.

You may have heard the terms *frequency* and *vibration* alongside *energy*. If you've ever wondered what they mean, the definitions are pretty straightforward. Vibration is simply the intensity, or the amplitude, of energy, and it exists as a kind of rhythmic pattern. Frequency is the rate at which energy vibrates, usually measured in hertz (Hz), which is equal to one cycle per second.

Vibrations and frequencies occur on both a macrocosmic and microcosmic level. For example, our planet's natural frequency, which cocoons the entire biosphere and all living beings, is known as the Schumann resonance, and has a rate of 7.83 Hz. Our heartbeats, breathing patterns, and circadian rhythms also have measurable vibrations and frequencies. On a nanoscale, at the level of atomic and subatomic particles, there are vibrations that generate electromagnetic energy, which can effect change on a cellular level.

Amazingly, energy, vibration, and frequency don't exist only on the level of physical matter; they also correspond to thoughts and beliefs, creating demonstrable patterns in the body (like an increased or decreased heartbeat or breathing pattern). Some metaphysicians and even physicists have theorized that changing our thoughts, behaviors, and the external stimuli in our environment can actually alter the vibrations and frequencies within our cells and DNA. This impacts how energy flows through us, which can have a substantial impact on our emotional, mental, and physical health.

Basically, when it comes to the nonmaterial aspects of our reality, modern science is starting to catch up to what the ancients knew.

T. M. Srinivasan is a physicist who has worked extensively on investigating holistic concepts like yoga, consciousness, and subtle energy—any energy that might be at a low or even unmeasurable intensity, meaning it can't be measured by physical instruments. His research focuses on gaining a scientific understanding of energy medicine, defined as any "energetic" interaction with a biological system that brings an organism back into equilibrium or its natural state. Energy medicine encompasses mind/body medicine, biologically based practices, manipulative body-based practices, and whole medical systems.

One thing all of these systems share is the idea that subtle energy is what sustains and promotes all the processes inside the body. These energies include those we learn about in physics: strong and weak nuclear forces, and gravitational and electromagnetic forces. But subtle energy also includes that which can't be measured, such as prayer. While there are studies that prove the efficacy of prayer and therapeutic touch, we still can't measure the subtle energy behind these activities.

But there are ways to indirectly measure subtle energy. For example, Kirlian photography is a technique that captures and measures the "aura," or subtle energy body, that surrounds an organism's physical body. The colors observed in the aura correspond to the function of the organs. Although Kirlian photography is still questioned in the scientific community, I think it's time to open our minds to these forms of measuring energy. After all, not even the smartest computer scientists in the world know exactly how artificial intelligence works. That's because the kind of generative AI we see today is so complex that humans can't easily comprehend or understand the step-by-step processes of its decision-making. Does that mean AI doesn't exist? Obviously not! It just means we don't understand all the details of how it works.

I encourage you to keep an open mind as you explore the practices in this book and their effect on your baseline energy. By expanding this energy, your biological, mental, and subtle processes are optimized in ways that help you achieve what you might have previously believed impossible.

important

Again, you don't need to have any kind of belief system in particular to do these practices—you can talk to angels or be a card-carrying atheist, and you'll get the same results. That's because energy is real, and the methods in this book will teach you to work with and transform it in ways that shift your mindset and your reality.

Sure, the most hardcore skeptics might get results from the practices and still boil it down to coincidence, which is fine with me. But you won't know until you try!

MORE RESOURCES AND FREE DOWNLOADS

Enhance your connection to your energetic body! Download the **Energy Awareness Reflection Guide** to explore how your energy shifts throughout the day. Use this simple practice every morning and night to strengthen your energy hygiene. Download here:

https://dothisbeforebed.com/resource

CHAPTER 2

THE POWER OF ROUTINES

I encourage you to make the four foundational practices a regular part of your bedtime routine. In the same way we brush and floss every night, practicing energy hygiene is fundamental to our overall health.

We know from research that routines can be an essential part of improving our health. Although routines might seem kind of boring and labor-intensive, they actually make life easier for us in the long run. They help build healthy habits that support us far into the future. They also help us manage stress, sleep more soundly, and choose healthier options for ourselves with respect to things like food and exercise. Routines kickstart our life into gear and enable us to take our lives into our own hands. They empower us to take small but necessary steps toward our dreams—and to also gain clarity on what's important to us, based on the results we achieve.

So, you might be wondering: *If routines are so awesome, why is it so hard to stick to them?* Instead of forming healthy habits through committed routines, why do most of us end up incessantly scrolling social media, or watching Netflix, or simply allowing our time to be swallowed by things that don't necessarily make us any better or wiser?

I believe that we give routines short shrift because we're worried it'll take too much effort to blend them into our daily lives despite the physical, emotional, mental, and energetic benefits they offer. I've heard the "it'll take too much work" excuse a lot over the last 20 years. I've come to realize that this belief conceals an even bigger self-sabotaging belief that keeps us from establishing routines: *Change can feel threatening.*

When we make the excuse that a bedtime routine is too much work, that's usually just a cover for the truth. We're afraid of what might happen if we move toward healthy, habit-forming routines. It might seem a little strange to think of positive change as being threatening, but if we've grown accustomed to life being a little dull and lackluster—well, at least we have predictability! Healthy change inevitably means leveling up, which can surface all kinds of insecurities for some people.

If you're feeling some of those insecurities come up right now, please don't worry. You might be deathly afraid of change or think that you're too lazy to establish a meaningful routine. You're welcome to bring all those beliefs along for the ride. The techniques in this book, starting with the four foundational practices, are going to help you blast through any insecurities and find yourself smooth sailing the seas of your own destiny. Because this book is about transforming your beliefs—but not necessarily by replacing them with other beliefs. Instead, you'll discover that your beliefs naturally change when you make the foundational practices a habit. When you build a powerful enough bedtime routine, you begin expanding the scope of what's possible. You also start to naturally grow beyond your comfort zone, so that what was once uncomfortable becomes something you enthusiastically and effortlessly find yourself stepping into.

In other words, don't be intimidated. None of this is designed to be hard! And establishing a routine doesn't mean everything has to be set in stone and you can't go off-road. I know so many people who have decided that the path of inner work and healing isn't for them because they think it needs to be done a certain way. The truth is, the sky's the limit and all roads lead to Rome. You can absolutely break the rules when it comes to designing a routine that works for you, especially if it means getting to where you want to go by taking the short-cut—which can be the more fun and scenic route.

Speaking of which, in the spiritual world, one of the routines people are most encouraged to adopt is meditation. Hence, one of the most common questions I get from students and clients, especially when it comes to developing a bedtime routine that serves their personal and spiritual growth, is: "Do I have to meditate?"

My answer is always, "It depends."

I know people who are pretty hardcore about their meditation practice; for example, I've met monks and spiritual teachers who engage in at least two to three hours of meditation a day.

I also meet everyday people who go through intense periods of devotion to their meditation practice. For example, maybe someone goes on a life-changing ten-day meditation retreat. Subsequently, they're inspired to meditate for several weeks or months before the practice dwindles and life takes over. What I've discovered is that, for most people, a regular daily meditation practice isn't sustainable. Personally, it has never truly resonated or worked for me in such a way that I've ended up incorporating it into my own daily routines. So, when students come to me with this question, I always remind them it's not an either/or, and everyone's different! If meditation resonates with you and you can do it with as sustained a focus as possible, you'll probably experience positive results.

I do believe that meditation for the purpose of entering into a state of deep relaxation, in which your mind isn't swimming with incessant thoughts, is one vehicle to take you into your desired results, or at least an altered state of consciousness that can open you up to possibility. However, I know plenty of people who experience meditative effects without meditating. For example, some people love running, yoga, or even cleaning their house because they're releasing a lot of energy when they do these activities. Thus, they end up receiving the same clearing and cleansing benefits that meditation can offer.

If you feel that your energetic makeup is such that you just can't get into meditation, don't feel guilty or like you're not creating enough discipline around your personal development. Also, keep in mind that things are always in flux, and it's okay to change your mind. You might find yourself gravitating to meditation in the future. I also know people who used to love meditating, but at some point, it stopped feeling meaningful or productive to them. That usually means they've outgrown it, and it's time to explore a new pathway for personal development.

Once again, allow me to stress that *meditation is just one vehicle* for helping you achieve clarity or create space for a positive mindset or the influx of creative ideas. Thoughts and energy have emotions attached to them, and these emotions get stuck in the physical and energetic body. While meditation will work for some, movement is a more effective way to release that energy for other people. Whatever the case, consider the kind of person *you* are. Maybe you're someone who benefits from vigorous activity, or maybe you require more calming techniques for cooling down your nervous system. There are no shoulds! Do what feels right for you, and the rest will naturally follow.

MORE RESOURCES AND FREE DOWNLOADS

Get into the flow with routines that support your energy! Download the **Daily Energy Routine Checklist** to help you establish powerful, energy-boosting habits even on your busiest days. Download here:

https://dothisbeforebed.com/resource

CHAPTER 3

SET YOURSELF UP FOR SUCCESS

Making the foundational practices a regular part of your bedtime routine is a great way to maintain a rigorous record of any tangible changes you notice in your life—and I promise you will! However, since we already know how tough it can be to get the ball rolling on our routines, there's still a little prework I suggest doing in order to set yourself up for success. A lot of us understandably feel drained by the time we hit the hay, which is why we usually want to just zone out—but there are lots of things we can do to clear away the cobwebs and optimize this sacred time of day. To that end, setting your space energetically and physically is crucial.

It takes most people a little extra time to settle down before they can get to sleep.* Your practices will take about 20 to 30 minutes (at least at first—after you've worked with this protocol for a minimum of 30 days, you can reduce the amount of time you spend on the foundational practices to five to ten minutes). So, before you retreat to your bedtime sanctuary, be sure to keep a mental note of whether there's anything you need to wrap up before bed.

---

* I acknowledge that insomnia and other sleep-related disorders are now more prevalent than ever before, so it's important to note that not everyone is able to sleep at night for a number of reasons—for example, medical personnel on 36-hour shifts, third-shift workers, and people with specific health issues might not have a typical sleep schedule. While sleeping in alignment with the circadian rhythm is optimal, I recognize that not everyone has the same sleep routine. That's perfectly okay; you can use the practices in this book whenever they work best for you, and in alignment with your own personal rhythms.

For example, if your body is holding excess energy, you might need to go for a walk or do some simple yoga stretches. Maybe you need to take a shower in order to wash off the grime and excess of the day. Perhaps you can let your partner or kids or the other people around you know that you're not to be disturbed for the next half hour. If you keep electronics around, you may want to turn off your cellphone or place it in another room so it won't take away your focus. I also find it useful to set boundaries around things like work, which can serve as a major distraction (more about this in Chapter 7). I used to respond to e-mails and texts from my team and students at all hours of the day, but I've reined in that habit. If it's after 5 P.M., I know it can usually wait until morning!

Basically, it's a good idea to consider all the things that may serve as distractions (and I know we all have our own unique set of distractions, in addition to the usual suspects) and strategically find ways to put them aside!

I often work with people who tell me it's hard to establish a routine because they sleep in the same bed as a partner who has vastly different ideas of how they want to spend the last chunk of their day. My response: That's fine, as long as you find a respectful way to communicate your needs (for example, maybe they can watch the football game silently on their iPad while you get into your practices). You do you!

Obviously, it's ideal that the people closest to you are doing the practices as well (there's a reason people team up with exercise buddies to get in a consistent workout!), but it's not necessary. The purpose of these practices is to help you strengthen *your* capacity to deal with *your* busy internal and external worlds. The practices are bound to have ripple effects on everyone you come in contact with. But work on you first.

If there's resistance from the people in your life, that can actually be a positive thing! It stretches your muscles, builds your tolerance, and challenges you to persevere in the face of obstacles. So, don't worry if your partner is resistant—nine out of ten times, my clients and students will tell me their partner eventually came around when they witnessed their transformations. When you strengthen your own energetic system, your embodied example is going to inspire others to want to do the same.

Another thing: I encourage you to open your mind up to what progress looks like. Sometimes, it will be dramatic; other times, it will be subtle. The important part is celebrating both the big and small changes in your life, and actually recognizing the places where you have shifted and where life has opened up more possibilities and opportunities than you imagined to exist.

While I know that anyone who does the foundational practices with regularity will see results, they have another important function: they help you acknowledge the blessings *when* they show up.

Often, people are unable to maintain routines because they aren't receiving instant gratification. This is why so many end up falling off the bandwagon and quitting altogether, even though they might just be starting to make big shifts—which may look and feel imperceptible. As you work with the tools, you'll begin to build greater and greater sensitivity, meaning you'll perceive and appreciate the subtle changes that add up to dramatic shifts. And I guarantee—they happen very quickly.

Like I said before, I like to get results *fast*. However, the kinder and more flexible we can be, the longer we can sustain the practices and the more reliably we'll see results. As I'll teach you, it's all a matter of taking notice of all the *good* things that are happening right now, breathing in the gifts you're receiving, noticing the signs and synchronicities that come your way, and making the practices such a fundamental way of life that miracles can't help but come in through the open doors of your mind and heart.

MORE RESOURCES AND FREE DOWNLOADS

Prepare for success with mindful relaxation! Download the **Guided Nighttime Routine Meditation Audio** to help you unwind and set the tone for a restful night, optimizing your sleep and energy for the day ahead. Listen here:

https://dothisbeforebed.com/resource

CHAPTER 4

THE FOUR FOUNDATIONAL PRACTICES

One of the things that makes life so challenging for many people is that they are walking around with an inherited set of beliefs that don't make them any healthier, happier, or more connected to themselves and others. The foundational practices will help you become more attuned to the real you—the eternal you who existed way before your mind and heart were taken over by limiting beliefs and ideas about who you are and how reality operates. As you get into a rhythm with them, you'll gain a greater sense of clarity that helps you connect to your highest needs, and the beliefs that actually support you to tap into your full potential.

For example, these days I don't necessarily end my evening with all the practices if I'm in my house in Colorado, in a town of 800 people—because the beautiful natural environment and peaceful setting ends up clearing any residual negative or chaotic energy that might be lingering in the air. However, if I'm traveling to a city like Los Angeles or New York, then I'm around lots of people or situations that might be energy-draining or triggering, as well as being exposed to external stimuli that may affect my well-being. On those occasions, I might double up on the foundational practices by doing them in the morning and the evening.

I recommend going all in with the foundational practices at first, maybe even doing them repeatedly throughout the day so you can build a higher level of mastery. This will help you develop a more intuitive sense of what you need over time. As I said, if these four practices are all you take from this book, that's great. You'll definitely notice a huge shift in your energy levels, mood, connection to yourself and others, and your ability to optimize your time and energy throughout the day.

Have fun, and sweet dreams!

#1: Clear and Open Your Third Eye, Ears, and Heart

If you're reading this book, I'm willing to bet you're probably sensitive to other people's energies, meaning you can feel it when someone else is anxious or overwhelmed, but also when they're happy and relaxed. It's likely that the energy centers in your body (also known as the chakras) are open, which is great! But the downside may be that these energy centers are overactive. If so, you could be bringing all that heightened energy into your sleep. That might be okay if you're mostly hanging out with a lot of enlightened, happy, peaceful, relaxed people! But the truth is, highly sensitive people are usually picking up on both obvious and not-so-obvious vibes. And, given the fact that we don't exactly live in a generally relaxed society, if you're highly sensitive, you may be carrying excess negativity and anxiety into your sleep—which you most certainly don't want to do!

During sleep, you're supposed to recharge and refuel. But if you're carrying other people's energy, you're more likely to have nightmares, astral travel to dark and heavy places, and wake up feeling drained, overwhelmed, and as if you didn't get a lick of sleep. So, for starters, right before you go to bed I encourage you to never fixate on people who triggered or hurt you.

very important!! →

This first tool focuses on setting an intention to release any negative energy you might have absorbed throughout the day. By doing so, you'll be taking back the sacred period of time that constitutes your sleep—a time for healing, recharging, rejuvenating, getting information, and connecting with your higher self. The three steps of this practice will help you to release any negative energy so you can experience the kind of peaceful calm essential to generate miracles.

Step 1: Release the Debris of the Day from Your Third Eye

step one!!

Your third eye is a powerful energy center that activates your intuition. You don't want negative, lower-level energies polluting it, so you want to first clear out the influences of the day by releasing toxic energies from it. Say to yourself, "I'm ready to release whatever is draining my third eye of energy and vitality, and to bring in my intuitive power and highest vision." Imagine white light (some people may resonate more with a violet or gold light) coming down from the skies, sending all the gunk in your third eye outside of you with a giant whoosh. Now, feel the light filling your third eye, rejuvenating and recharging it, and replacing it with positive, love-based energy.

Step 2: Clear Out Your Ears

step two!!

A lot of people don't realize that we also have energy centers in our ears, which, like the third eye, are constantly picking up words, thoughts, beliefs, and vibrations from others. You don't want this energy to invade your sacred slumber!

After you've cleared out your third eye, say to yourself, "I'm ready to release whatever is draining my ears of energy and vitality, and to bring in only the most loving words, thoughts, beliefs, and vibrations." Visualize that the same light as before is coming through your ears in the form of a little tornado, clearing out any harsh or unkind sentiments that infiltrated your ear chakras throughout the day. Now, imagine this light is brightening your ears, filling them with words and sounds of kindness and positivity.

Step 3: Unblock Your Heart of Toxic Attachments

Finally, it's time to unblock your heart of any toxic attachments that are making you feel disconnected from yourself and others. Your heart center is primarily where you store all the negative energy you've absorbed throughout the day. Your heart also has the largest and most powerful electromagnetic field in your body—so you want to make sure it's clear of any negative influences. After you've cleared out your ear chakras, say to yourself, "I'm ready to release whatever is draining my heart of energy and vitality, and to bring in love, joy, and rejuvenation." At this point, feel that same light you imagined whirling around your heart center, pulling out any toxic influences and making your heart shine bright and strong.

#2: Raise Your Vibration with Three Questions

It's so important to raise your vibration—which will make you feel like you can move mountains—and it's even more important to raise your vibration before you go to bed. I've found that this practice can be especially effective when it comes to turning your thoughts into reality. In fact, I've seen students and clients manifest what they want within 24 to 48 hours of doing this practice!

When you're in a high vibration, you attract other high-vibration people, situations, and experiences. All you have to do is ask yourself three simple questions:

1. What am I grateful for?

2. What did I do right today?

3. What experiences do I wish to create, and what emotions do I want to accompany those experiences?

For the first two questions, focus on simple joys, even if you had a really bad day: "I'm grateful I have a roof over my head. I'm grateful for the air I'm breathing. There wasn't any traffic on my morning commute. My boss complimented my work. My daughter told me the advice I gave her meant a lot." As you reflect on these questions, you'll feel both a sense of peace and excitement for all the beautiful things that are coming your way. Next thing you know, this high-vibrational energy will accumulate and flow into the next day, and you'll start experiencing more of what you want.

#3: Find the Higher Meaning

Sometimes, at the end of the day, we might feel discouraged about something that happened as if a door slammed shut on our fingers instead of opened with grace and welcome. We all experience disappointment, but this practice will help you transmute disappointment into possibility:

What's the higher meaning of this?

When "bad" things happen, it's easy to feel punished. But it's crucial to reframe these events. Consider how what you perceive as a disappointment might actually be leading you to the life you desire. Maybe the person who broke up with you, who seemed like such a good fit, is moving out of the way so your heart can make room for your true soulmate. Maybe your car stalling and making you late for an important meeting is a reminder to slow down and smell the roses instead of constantly overworking yourself.

Be open to the idea that what's happening in your life is exactly what you asked for, even if it doesn't seem like it. It's making space for the new you who's emerging . . . who'll be here faster than you think. If you're in pain, it's not permanent. For example, if you're suffering the loss of a relationship, what you often can't see in the moment is that this opens the door to a truer love. In a lot of cases, our pain breaks open our hearts to deeper compassion, understanding, and wisdom, as well—as long as we have faith that there's a purpose to it all. So, have faith that there is a higher meaning, and that what you want is right around the corner.

key

#4: Connect with the You Who Has It All

key

The final foundational practice is perhaps the most powerful, so I encourage you to spend the most time with it. In fact, if you do this three nights in a row, your life will never be the same! *Do This every night . . . .*

There's a version of you right now who has it all. This version of you exists in the quantum field of possibility and is already living your best life with all the abundance, joy, peace, love, and wellness you could imagine. So, after working through the first three practices, I want you to set a simple intention. Say to yourself, "I choose to connect to the highest version of me, the one who has it all." *Very important!*

Next, imagine white light pouring down from the sky, going through your head and filling your entire body. Follow the light as far as you can go, beyond the edges of Earth and the solar system. Go to the very end of this cosmic light, and then beyond. Sense that your higher self is here, living the life of your dreams.

Do this!!

Don't feel the need to force anything. You don't even have to visualize all the things you want, although you are free to do so. Just let yourself be bathed in the energy of this glorious version of you. At first, your experience might feel subtle or even a little awkward. Just stick with it, and I promise you'll come to understand why this exercise is so awesome. Most people don't receive images in this place. It's likely that the energy of the highest version of you will come through sensations, feelings, or just a sense that you're connecting with something bigger than you.

Key!!

As you make these foundational practices an intrinsic part of your life, everything will change. You may find yourself seeing, hearing, and sensing the loving presence of your highest self. Bathe in that vibration, allowing it to change you—because it will. I personally love falling asleep in this state, because I usually wake up with a greater sense of connection to that version of me. This only ends up magnetizing even more of what I want—and sometimes, miracles I didn't even think to ask for!

MORE RESOURCES AND FREE DOWNLOADS

Master the four foundations of energy work! Download the **Guided Energy Cleansing Meditation Audio** to walk you through the foundational practices and clear your energy before bed. Listen here:

https://dothisbeforebed.com/resource

PART 2

TOOLS FOR HEALING AND MANIFESTATION

So many of my clients and students struggle with chronic stress and other issues that set off a domino effect of conditions, leaving them to feel broken down and defeated. Instead of succumbing to this avalanche of internal and external challenges, you have the ability to create greater clarity that will empower you to find solutions to the larger problems you might be facing.

This part of the book empowers you to "heal thyself," which has a ripple effect on your life and the world around you—creating greater space for love, forgiveness, happiness, and the clarity to move forward without the baggage of the past weighing you down.

In the remaining chapters of this book, you'll be offered tools to clear away any debris that's interfering with constructing the metaphorical house of your dreams. You'll clear old beliefs that are hijacking your present happiness and unclog blockages in your physical/emotional/spiritual health. In addition, you'll find practices that will accelerate your efforts to manifest the life of your dreams. But just remember that healing and manifestation go hand-in-hand. It can be challenging to manifest what you want when the space for dreaming your desires into being is blocked by beliefs and habits that don't serve you. By the same token, it can be hard to maintain the stamina to clear internal blockages when you don't feel you're getting any traction with your manifestation efforts.

Here, you'll find practices that encompass finding life-changing love, healing trauma, making the best of life transitions, optimizing physical health and wellness, transforming mental fog, harnessing the clarity to make a difficult decision, establishing boundaries, increasing self-esteem, and resetting your body and mind as you sleep. Once you've made the foundational practices a daily tool, you can go through this section at the pace you feel most comfortable with—and you can get started immediately!

Please know none of this is about getting it "perfect" or "right"; it's more about noticing how the practices make you feel, as well as the changes that they elicit in your life. Your learning process and evolution are your own, and everyone is going to connect with the practices in their own unique way, based on what they need to learn. In addition, your motive for moving through the practices in this section doesn't have to be noble or altruistic. I'm not here to change you or what you want. Often, my social-media videos that tend to go viral are centered around seemingly frivolous topics, such as, "How do I get my ex back or make them fall in love with me again? How do I deal with drama in the workplace? How do I find the perfect place to live?" In many ways, my work comes in under the guise of helping people get what they most desire—but what they're actually getting is freedom: to *think* different, *act* different, and *be* different.

No matter what it is you're looking for, the practices in this section will help you orient toward greater alignment with yourself, which means your initial goals may naturally end up shifting along the way as you gain greater clarity and learn to create more space for what will truly fulfill you.

CHAPTER 5

ABUNDANCE AND MANIFESTATION

If there's one thing my students and clients are eager to learn about, it's the mechanics of generating abundance and manifesting what they most want. There are tons of textbook definitions for *manifestation*, but I think of it as "bending time." That is, manifestation is *the acceleration of the rate at which abundance can arrive at your doorstep*.

Many people feel the life of their dreams will take ages to drop onto their doorstep. This is primarily because they are operating under the mistaken belief that they have to "do" something (get the right degree, move to the right location, find the right partner, etc.) in order to manifest what they want. This is an outdated way of looking at manifestation, and I promise you it can be so much easier. With the right approach to manifestation, what may seem like it's far away can happen in a nanosecond, and it doesn't require huge amounts of effort. In fact, effective manifestation is about adopting a high-vibration, miracle-oriented mindset.

I always teach my students that there are two ways of manifesting: *low vibration* and *high vibration*.

Let's first take a look at low-vibration manifesting. When we are in a low vibration, we are operating from the status quo of our human identity; we're swirling in emotions like fear, anger, anxiety, and insecurity, and we're trying really, *really* hard! In essence, we're still swimming in the energetic muck, which is against the natural current of abundance. We might want love but we're afraid of getting hurt; we might want a prestigious career but we're afraid of being successful. We are attached to numerous hindrances and torn apart by all kinds of inner conflicts. Let me be clear: It's absolutely possible to manifest from such a place (I've done it, and so have plenty of people I know), but this tends to be either slow manifestation—or, if it happens, it doesn't last long and comes at a price.

Low-vibration manifesting is a muddy and polarizing way to manifest, because it comes from a tendency to divide our experiences into "good" and "bad." That's because low-vibration manifesting operates under the rules of humanity—dictated by control and fear—rather than the rules of the soul, which is centered around expansion, unity, and abundance.

As I mentioned in the prior chapter, I've had many clients and students come to me with questions like, "How do I get my ex back?" or, "How do I avoid getting evicted?" They are focused on reacting to wounds and rejection, or running from pain, or trying to prove themselves, or attempting to get validation from the external world. When you manifest from this place, your mindset is ruled by duality. It's like a twisted version of Newton's third law of motion: for every awesome thing that happens, there's an equal and opposite crappy thing that'll accompany it.

For example, I had a student, Shannon, who succeeded in getting her ex back—which was why she came to study with me in the first place! She was stuck in low-vibration manifesting that came from low self-esteem and the belief formed in childhood that she would always be abandoned. So, even though she was focused on what she *wanted* (which many manifestation experts assert is enough to get it), her underlying belief was that good times would soon be followed by bad times, and the other shoe would most certainly drop. Well, what do you think she ended up manifesting? Her ex came back, but in this toxic iteration of their relationship, he cheated on her, which left Shannon even more heartbroken than before.

Shannon learned that the place we manifest from often determines the kinds of results we get—and that low-vibration manifesting brings all our baggage and low-vibe tendencies: self-sabotage, worry, fear, feeling we don't deserve a good life, etc. All this was a major wake-up call for Shannon, and she was finally ready to learn about and practice high-vibration manifesting.

High-vibration manifesting, as I've mentioned, operates by the rules of the soul, which orients us toward the abundance we already have and allows us to feel excited about what could be. Instead of fixating on something we want from a place of lack or of needing external evidence of our worthiness, we come from a brand-new state of flow, gratitude, and surrender.

Shannon did the foundational practices for a few weeks, and I noticed a shift in her energy and how she showed up. When I first met her, she had downcast eyes that never met my gaze, and shoulders sloped down in a posture of defeat. Over time, she had more pep in her step and was more cheerful and confident. I coached Shannon to think about what she wanted and how it would make her feel. Her face lit up and her eyes became bright. "I'm ready for a love that's uplifting. I'm ready to feel connected on the level of my soul. I'm ready for someone who can meet me in such a way that we're both eager to travel the road of life together and to make discoveries that change us for the better, and that help us contribute to the well-being of others."

I was impressed by the clarity of Shannon's intentions, which revealed that she was coming from a mindset of high-vibration manifestation. It was a huge shift from the desperation she'd brought into her first manifestation! I encouraged her to lightly hold that intention as she worked with the three practices you'll learn in this chapter. Not surprisingly, about two weeks later, a message from a kind and attractive man she'd met in a yoga class more than a year ago slid into her DMs, and the rest is history! Shannon met the love of her life and is now happily teaching other women the value of raising their vibration to have greater joy and fulfillment.

If you're someone who feels your belief system is full of negativity that you may have inherited from your upbringing or other life experiences, it's possible to change your vibration on a dime. (Which is where the second foundational practice—Raise Your Vibration with Three Questions—*really* comes in. Once you practice it on a daily basis for at least a month, you'll see what I mean!) Vibration can be impacted by beliefs, for sure, but it's also extremely fluid. I've met lots of people who've "accidentally" manifested great things in their life. They usually think of it as a random fluke, but what actually occurred is that they unknowingly hit a high vibration, maybe through something like a simple meditation practice or by doing an activity that got them out of their heads and into their hearts—both of which can promote high-vibration states.

This ain't about being perfect! Our old wounds might still be unhealed in the moment we manifest, but it's only when we're actively triggered or swirling in our pain that we manifest from a low-vibration state. At the same time, I always encourage my clients and students to expand their beliefs to the best of their ability. It's not about just saying, "Okay, I won't believe that I'm unworthy anymore," which usually doesn't work. It's about adding to our "bag of tools" by forming new beliefs that gradually eclipse the old ones. This is what Shannon did when she used the foundational practices: she developed a connection with her higher self that helped her step into a natural state of confidence and openness.

key

Remember, you can truly manifest anything from either a low or high vibration, but also consider: How are you going to *feel* when you get that thing you want? Will you be happy? Will you be able to enjoy your manifestation without self-sabotaging? In general, it's a lot harder to do this from a low vibration, or when we have hidden negative beliefs that momentarily get shrouded by a high-vibe moment.

Another question I often get from people is: Should I be focused on manifesting general or specific things?

I've done both, but I've realized that when I want something specific—such as a particular opportunity, or a material object—it's hit or miss and not very predictable. My theory is that while my mind is holding this very clear idea of what I want, my soul is waiting for me to release the idea (surrender is the most important ingredient in high-vibration manifesting, which can often occur very quickly, especially if we genuinely let go of the outcome) so that the universe can do its thing. It's a lot harder to release your specific intended outcome than it is to release a more generalized outcome.

For example, there were times I said to myself, "It would be really nice to attract a business partnership that feels soul-nourishing and that helps me to level up my game and feel even more connected to my higher self—and I invite whatever wants to come, for the highest good of all," without having any idea what this partnership could or should be! And then, lo and behold, the opportunity ends up coming when I'm flowing in a high-vibration state: for example, in the middle of teaching a workshop and being in a space of service.

key "High vibration state"

31

Try it for yourself. I encourage you to use the practices below to work with manifesting both general and specific outcomes. Stay open to whatever comes, and recognize that your vibration makes all the difference!

My favorite time to manifest is in the wee hours, between sleeping and waking; the state that occurs just before falling asleep is known as the hypnagogic state, and the state that occurs just after waking up is known as the hypnopompic state. People ranging from Aristotle to Edison and Einstein knew all about the power of these liminal phases—and more importantly, they knew that during these times, a person is connected to their higher power and is capable of harnessing an unlimited amount of creative energy. During these times, thoughts become things extremely quickly—especially when you remember to home in on your intention. So, I encourage you to practice the following exercises when you're in that high-potential space of the in-between!

THE PRACTICES

#1: Surrender and Receive

I've worked with a lot of people who struggle with their capacity to receive the highest and best things in life. Many people carry unconscious beliefs about their unworthiness, which can make it hard to receive all the goodness that life has in store for us.

If you operate under the assumption that what you seek is also seeking you, what if it's already on its way to you? That means love, joy, abundance, and all the things you want in life are on their way, and the only reason you're not experiencing them right now is because you're not open to receiving.

I Am open to Receiving ↑

By reciting the following statement, you open up to grace and increase your ability to receive. I encourage you to try it for at least three nights straight, and watch the blessings flood in!

Put your hand over your heart and silently say the words below, which you can also write down on a piece of paper that you keep under your pillow, or keep as a note in your phone:

Everything I want comes to me quickly, easily, and effortlessly.
I am taken care of and I am provided for.

Miracles and blessings pour into my life.

Abundance is waiting for me when I wake up.

I am open. I am ready. I now receive
fully with an open heart.

Everything I need is already on its way to me.

I receive, I receive, I receive.

Thank you.

Every night speak this...

#2: Elevate Your Manifestation

I often have people who come to me with material concerns—like needing more money, or a car, or a place to live. I don't knock those desires. We live in a material world, and it's important that we feel our needs are adequately met, which can help us shift into a higher vibration. However, if you're in a place where you're focused on manifesting something for material comfort, there's a simple way to elevate the vibration behind your desire.

Let's say you want a nicer car. You don't have to stop there! Get into visualizing, sensing, and feeling the kinds of experiences you'd have if your desire were already fulfilled. What else would you be doing? Where would you be

major key !!

going? Who would you be going with? Whose lives would be elevated by virtue of you having a nicer car? How would all this make you feel?

When you elevate your intention with a higher meaning—such as, "I get to have adventures and take lots of other people along with me, which means we'll all be having so much fun and feeling so much connection"—this automatically puts you into a high vibration and allows you to experience higher-quality emotions, like gratitude, excitement, and joy. Shannon experienced this right before manifesting the love of her life. So, don't stop with the thing you want—get superclear about how it'll make you feel and how many lives it'll enrich if you get it!

For at least the next three nights, focus on one thing you want to manifest. Then, for three to five minutes, add plenty of reasons for why you want it and how it will make you feel once you have it. Let those reasons be expansive and for the highest good of all, and watch your dreams come true!

#3: Ask for Your Soul Lessons

Moving from a low to high vibration has a lot to do with learning important soul lessons. For example, I have students coming to my workshops wanting to manifest certain opportunities, but nothing's happening. One student, Cade, who wanted to build his coaching practice, revealed that he was in an ongoing relationship with a toxic person who made him second-guess his dreams. Obviously, this was distressing for him and lowered his vibration. We worked on helping Cade build the courage to stand in his power and speak his truth; when he did this, the relationship ended, but he was able to establish a six-figure coaching practice where his deeper gifts could finally shine.

If you've ever felt like you've been spinning your wheels and remaining stationary instead of making headway with your manifestation, there's probably something that's lowering your vibration. Often, it's one or more predictable, simple human constructs—like a toxic relationship, or a habit of clamping down on your truth, or a health issue you haven't addressed—keeping you stuck and holding you back.

For the next three nights, state your desire to yourself. Put your request out there, and then let it go. Now, ask yourself: "What are the soul lessons I most need to learn right now?" Another way of asking this is: "What do I need to express in my life in order to move into a higher vibration?"

Let the answer arise without forcing it; let it come from your heart, not your head. The soul lesson might be gratitude, or presence, or forgiving yourself or someone else. It might be setting a boundary with someone who is not respectful, or being vulnerable, or being unafraid to shine. It might be taking a baby step in the direction of your dream career, which will signal to the universe that you're ready and receptive. Whatever the case, not expressing the soul lesson that your heart identifies is lowering your vibration and causing blockages.

Now, occasionally, I come across people who have difficulty with this exercise because they feel everything in their life is an obstacle, and there's not just one thing that's contributing to their low vibration. If this is the case for you, it's crucial that you take action to change the ratio of "negative" to "positive." For example, what are you being exposed to? Who are your friends? What kind of media are you taking in? Our external world has the power to change our internal world, so I encourage people swamped in low vibes to shift their lives, bit by bit, by turning up the volume on positivity. If you have four friends who are negative and complain a lot, and just one friend with a bright outlook, you'll want to spend 80 percent of your effort and energy on that one friendship. Developing systems and environments of support help sustain your manifestation; it's like soaking in newer, higher vibes through osmosis and immersion—which is crucial if you want your nighttime manifestation practices to take off!

[handwritten margin note: "major"]

MORE RESOURCES AND FREE DOWNLOADS

Manifest abundance while you sleep! Listen to the **Manifestation Meditation Audio** to amplify your abundance mindset and attract what you desire during restful sleep. Listen now:

https://dothisbeforebed.com/resource

CHAPTER 6

ADVENTURE, FUN, AND PLAY

A lot of people come to the world of "personal development" with all kinds of goals, from stress reduction to building a successful business to deepening their spiritual practices. The one thing that constantly surprises me is that few people I meet say, "I'm here because I want to have more fun and adventure in my life!"

Obviously, there's way more to life than just having fun, but it's a lopsided approach we're taking if we don't factor in enjoyment! Joy is one of the most important high-vibration emotions to cultivate, and while it can come from a medley of experiences, we forget that our capacity for fun is a huge part of it. And when I'm talking about fun, I'm talking about the kinds of activities that make us feel our aliveness in the deepest ways—that encourage us to express and explore more of who we are.

We are meant to enjoy our lives, but this is something we forget to do as adults. It's a lot easier to cultivate a spirit of adventure and fun when we're kids. Practically everything is an opportunity for exploration, especially because we're like little sponges soaking up all that's in our midst. Unfortunately, as we get older, we become creatures of habit. We begin to get into structured routines (which are, no doubt, important when it comes to navigating our busy schedules) and form preferences that leave a lot less room for spontaneity . . . which means we habituate ourselves to activities that are mostly connected to work, family, and other responsibilities. Most adults limit themselves to adventure and fun on the weekends, or for the two weeks of vacation time they have saved up.

The great news is, you can still establish routines while leaving room for adventure and fun. Each of us is unique and our ideas of adventure and fun can vary greatly, but the key aspects it's important to look for are activities and experiences that allow you to feel the way you did when you were a kid: curious, alive, and excited about life.

A lot of times, when we have leisure time, we usually take it as an opportunity to rest—which is very important. The thing is, we forget to nourish ourselves with the kind of joyful stimulation that asks us to challenge ourselves, to see the world through fresh eyes, and to stop taking ourselves so darn seriously! This is why we need time to play—which can look like anything from a weekly pickleball date with friends, to a spontaneous dance party with your kids, to something as simple as taking a new route to work through a neighborhood you've never explored. According to Dr. Stuart Brown, the founder of the National Institute for Play, although play might seem kind of trivial, it's anything but. Play is a biological drive that helps us to expand our creativity, form strong social connections, solve problems, and feel confident.

As far as I'm concerned, it's possible to begin to set time in our schedule to prioritize adventure, fun, and play. One of my clients is a Hollywood actor who tends to film intensively for three to four months at a time, and it can be difficult for him to focus on anything beyond work, since his day is split between sleep and filming. However, he tries to schedule two to three "silly" things he can do throughout the day that serve to charge him up and help him to preserve his zest for life—otherwise, by his admission, he'd be depressed and antsy. I'm also a huge fan of Julia Cameron's *The Artist's Way*, a book that encourages readers to take themselves on a weekly artist date—a festive solo outing that puts our inner explorer in the driver's seat and ensures that we're going off-road instead of playing by the rules.

Sometimes, giving ourselves space for adventure, fun, and play is about challenging ourselves to move beyond our fixed ideas of who we are by doing things that might feel a little intimidating (going mountain climbing, or taking an improv theater class); other times, it's about simply slowing down to notice and appreciate the things we don't give ourselves time to notice (developing a relationship with the animals in our garden, or scrapbooking personal memorabilia we haven't looked at in years).

When I notice students and clients stuck in rigid patterns, I encourage them to spend time with children, which can be a powerful lesson in maintaining a sense of presence and realizing that anything in our life can be an opportunity for a mini-expedition into places and states of being that as adults we don't always give ourselves access to. Kids have full use of their imagination, which is a powerful tool. They know how to daydream and how to beat boredom. Boredom is usually the result of energy that's stagnant and underused; when we don't access that energy in ways that bring us a sense of joy and aliveness, this can lead to anxiety, depression, or other forms of mental and physical malaise. When we express this energy, it nourishes us and fills our cup, and we usually find that we have even more energy to give to other areas of our life.

important

Everyone wants to feel like they're the main character in their own life, and we do this by balancing out our "adult" life of work and responsibilities with a sense of play and possibility. This isn't about chasing the next peak experience or buying a one-way ticket to some exotic location, though; it's about learning how to be present in every moment so that we can feel more, laugh more, and soak up all the goodness and pleasure this life has to offer.

THE PRACTICES

#1: Circulate Stagnant Energy

Whenever you feel like you're in a rut—you're just not able to have fun or welcome new adventures into your life, and there's a sense of dullness or apathy that permeates your experiences—it's time to move some energy! It is difficult to be open to a more joyful way of approaching life if we're stuck in a rigid holding pattern, which can happen when we're approaching each day as if it were a giant to-do list. We can repattern ourselves once we release those stagnant ideas. Here are the steps to circulating stagnant energy, which should take no more than five minutes total:

1. At bedtime, take two to three minutes to do some "body rolls." That is, go through each part of your body (head, shoulders, arms, hands, hips, legs, and feet) and move it in a circular motion, both clockwise and counterclockwise. This should feel really good, as if you are releasing lots of pent-up energy.

2. Next, for two to three minutes, tap up and down your body (front, back, sides, up and

down your arms and legs, on your face
and head, etc.) for a couple minutes, which
stimulates your meridian points and releases
tension. If it feels good, you might choose to
add some energy and pressure to the tapping.

3. As you do all of this, say the affirmation, "I'm
welcoming more fun and pleasure into my
life," and visualize yourself doing activities
that are fun for you. If it feels difficult to
come up with anything, think about the
last time you really enjoyed yourself and
visualize a similar situation. You might also
choose to visualize doing something you've
never done before that sounds really fun (like
ballroom dancing, scuba diving, or singing at
a karaoke bar).

You may not feel any immediate effects beyond the fact
that these movements usually bring a sense of balance to the
body and emotions. However, beneath the surface, you're
moving a lot of old energy! The combination of physical
movement, verbal affirmation, and visualization is extremely
effective in anchoring a new state of being—that is, one of
receptivity to fun and pleasure.

#2: Cultivate a Childlike State of Mind

Remember what it was like to be a kid? Certainly, not all
of us (and probably not even most of us) had idyllic child-
hoods, but we can probably remember the feeling of wonder
that permeated our lives as we welcomed new experiences
and simply took in what the world had to share with us. As
children, we don't have the same rigid concepts that serve

to make our lives "safe" and predictable when we're adults. We're usually more curious and less judgmental.

At bedtime, take five minutes to reflect on the following questions:

1. What did you absolutely love when you were a child (e.g., jumping rope, dancing, playing on the swings, playing make-believe)?

2. Now, focus on one of the things you chose that you loved as a child. Why did you love it so much? For example, perhaps playing make-believe connected you to a more expansive reality that gave you a sense of connection to magic and mystery. You'll most likely have a few reasons, but focus on the one that feels the most relevant or alive.

3. Now, allow that feeling to get bigger so that it radiates through your entire being. For example, maybe that feeling is "connection to magic and mystery." You know what that feels like in your body. Do your best to hold it in your consciousness and your very cells for at least a couple minutes.

4. Next, let that feeling go and say the affirmation, "I trust the wise child within me."

In doing this exercise, you're activating that aspect of your essence that automatically knows what it loves, what brings it joy, what makes it come alive. This is a wonderful part to connect with whenever you want to feel more alive, especially in moments when you might feel tired, bored, or disenchanted with life.

I suggested to one of my students, Anne, that she try this for at least a week, during a time when she felt stressed out by the challenges of being a single mom. At first, she outright refused, "because I don't think this is going to help me." But when she let her curiosity get the better of her, within a week she actually *looked* different. Gone was the harried woman with tight shoulders and a frown on her face. She was jovial and full of laughter.

> *I'm not sure what exactly happened, she said, but I feel like I regained a spark I thought I'd lost. After a few days, I began waking up with more energy and a sense that there was something to look forward to. I haven't felt this way in a long time, but it really does seem as if the little girl I used to be is here, reminding me that I was made for way more than kvetching about overdue bills or my kids not doing their chores.*

Over time, this version of Anne became more and more prominent. Her sense of playfulness was contagious, and she discovered that more people (including her kids) wanted to be around her. The quality of Anne's life greatly improved, all because she was ready to step back into that childlike place of openness and discovery.

MORE RESOURCES AND FREE DOWNLOADS

Unlock your sense of adventure and joy! Listen to the **Inner Child Guided Meditation Audio** to reconnect with playfulness and fun in your daily life. Listen here:

https://dothisbeforebed.com/resource

CHAPTER 7

BOUNDARIES

One of the major topics of my workshops and the work I do with clients and students has to do with the power of setting a strong boundary. Our boundaries demarcate what we are saying yes and no to. If we're looking at things from an energetic perspective, we are infinite beings with a limitless array of possibilities; however, if we're looking at things from the vantage point of matter, we live within the constraints of three-dimensional bodies. What I've found is that when we get better at setting boundaries and making decisive choices in our 3D world, we actually start to access the superpowers of our infinite self.

When we set boundaries, we make important decisions about what we're choosing to give our time and energy to. Every decision we make, whether conscious or not, either amplifies or takes away from our sense of power. This is why it's so important for us to get into the habit of making conscious choices that support our deepest values and allow us to grow into the people we want to be.

The thing a lot of people misunderstand about boundaries is that they're not either-or, black or white. Boundaries are flexible protective mechanisms, not stone walls. When we don't get this, it can result in a lot of unnecessary pain. However, when we remember that there's an entire spectrum of possibilities available to us in setting a boundary, we can be really creative when it comes to instilling and enforcing our own. It can become a skillful game of negotiation, connection, and communication—not a defense that's meant to scare others away!

I once had a student named Carly who was a chronic people pleaser (or, in her description, a "well-worn, well-scuffed doormat!"). Carly grew up with two very demanding parents who had never given her space to say no. The message Carly had unconsciously absorbed was that she always had to give in to other people and do what they wanted her to do, or else she would be unloved. This had continued up to the present day. Carly was in over her head at work, as her boss had loaded a lot of extra responsibilities onto her plate. Now, she was doing the work of at least three employees.

Carly was a single mom of two kids who always seemed to manipulate her into letting them do whatever they wanted to. On top of all that, Carly's mom's health was in severe decline, and Carly's siblings expected her to take on the bulk of caregiving. Understandably, when Carly came to my classes, she was a nervous wreck. Her tendency to say yes all the time had taken a toll on her health, and she was dealing with adrenal fatigue and an anxiety that constantly buzzed in the background.

"Have you ever tried to set boundaries with your boss, kids, and siblings?" I asked.

She looked like a deer caught in the headlights. "I wouldn't know where to begin!"

I knew that asking Carly to draw some heavy lines in the sand would be way too much for her nervous system to handle, so I taught her the value of "yes, and." Carly didn't have to say no to any requests, but she could follow each yes with a request of her own. For example, when her boss wanted her to work late, if Carly felt that was a reasonable request, she could say something like, "Yes—and I'd like to take the following Monday off to balance out my overtime hours." Or if her kids insisted on eating sweets, she might say, "Yes—and you have to eat all your vegetables first." And if her siblings insisted that she be the one to take their mom to all her doctor's appointments, Carly could respond, "Yes, and I'd like for us to create a weekly schedule to help Mom with her day-to-day tasks, so that all of us can get a break when we need to."

Even the game of "yes, and" was tough for Carly—at least at first. I coached her through the process of rewiring her people-pleasing tendencies. A lot of times, when we're reluctant to say no—even if it's a soft no—it's a good idea to start asking ourselves, "Why don't I want to say no? What am I afraid of?"

Carly was afraid of hurting the people in her life—so I encouraged her to consider how, in dishonoring herself by saying yes when she didn't really want to, she was actually hurting others in a more subtle and insidious way. She was robbing them of the opportunity for greater connection and intimacy with her; by being truthful, she would be inviting more collaboration and ways to create win-win situations that served everyone, including herself.

I also asked Carly, "By saying yes to these other people, how are you saying no to yourself, your dreams, and the person you want to be?" This really got her wheels turning, so I encouraged her to make it a practice to say no at least once a day. She didn't have to be blunt or forceful; she could be soft but decisive at the same time.

Over time, especially with the practices in this chapter, Carly learned to take back and stand in her power. She ultimately decided to leave her job and start her own physical therapy practice, which had been a long-standing dream. Today, her kids are teenagers who work in her practice after school and do what they can to support their mom. And because Carly made it clear that she would not be taking on the burden of caring for her mom alone, she and her siblings were able to pool their resources together to get a full-time home healthcare nurse to do the bulk of the caregiving while ensuring that their mom has ample time with each of them. Today, Carly is happy and healthy, and her boundaries have given her the opportunity to build stronger relationships and prioritize her dreams and desires.

Through our work together, one of the most important things I taught Carly to get clear about, and that I always share with my students and clients, is that there are all kinds of boundaries we can start to make in our lives, some of which don't even require the buy-in of other people. Let's look at what they are.

- **Physical boundaries:** Physical boundaries are connected to the environments we find ourselves stepping into. For example, we might recognize that specific environments deplete our energy and make us feel disempowered. I have lots of clients and students who dislike being in big cities because of all the frenetic energy. We can't always avoid these experiences, but we can notice how we feel and accordingly determine what we will do in response. Carly realized that her original workplace, which was in a large office building with fluorescent lighting and no windows, made her feel depressed. This eventually helped her to transition into becoming her own boss. Now, the environment in which she works is open and airy, with lots of natural light and plants that make her feel happy and uplifted.

- **Time boundaries:** Many of us find ourselves in situations that drain our time. For example, perhaps you have a good friend who talks about himself all the time and doesn't let you get a word in edgewise. You value certain aspects of your connection, but maybe you realize the optimal way to spend time with him is to connect once every few months, and that you'll limit your interaction to an hour-long lunch.

- **Verbal boundaries:** Unlike physical and time boundaries, which may or may not be communicated to others, verbal boundaries are ones that have to be made explicit. They may or may not be nonnegotiable. For example, Carly told her kids that she needed an hour in the evening after work to decompress and "do nothing." She explained to them that if her door was closed, that meant she didn't want any interruptions unless it was an emergency. If Carly hadn't explicitly communicated her boundary to her kids, they wouldn't have any way of understanding *why* it was so important to her—and they certainly wouldn't have honored it.

- **Energetic boundaries:** Energetic boundaries are a little less obvious than the previously mentioned types. These are the ones we'll explore in more depth in the practices. We set an energetic boundary by simply setting an intention for ourselves, that we will not be depleted. Energetic boundaries are especially useful when we're feeling drained but we don't know exactly why. Often, the reason can be traced back to an experience of dishonoring our time, not stating a verbal boundary, or subjecting ourselves to a disempowering or challenging environment. However, we don't always know what might impact us— sometimes we figure it out a week later, after the fact. In addition, we're bombarded by so many different things these days—including advertising and social media—that it's not always possible to isolate the factors that are impacting us. This is why setting energetic boundaries at bedtime can be so powerful; we don't need to know whether or how we were impacted, but we can still set the intention that our time, energy, and other resources be protected and that we have ways to hit the reset button if we're feeling out of sorts.

Overall, when we set boundaries, we protect our vibration. It is possible to incorporate practices into our life that make our vibration our first defense against potential energetic drains. Carly raised her vibration so much that she seldom feels she needs to set the explicit boundaries she used to. This is because our vibration, when we get it to be high enough consistently enough, works wonders when it comes to magnetizing the situations that automatically fill us up with self-replenishing energy and keeping away the influences that might serve to deplete it.

THE PRACTICES

#1: Visualize Shrinking Your Aura

Your aura or your auric field is like your energetic skin—and just like your skin, it's capable of absorbing a lot of different kinds of energy. Unbeknownst to you, your aura may be overlapping with other people's auras—absorbing their thoughts, emotions, fears, and beliefs. This is a great practice to do the night before a big meeting or any kind of situation that would otherwise take you out of your center. It's also a great way to diffuse nervous energy and come back into your own body and energy.

Place a hand over your heart. Imagine yourself in the situation, picturing the people you'll be engaging with. Feel the radiance of your aura creating a protective shield around you that makes you feel confident, light, and easeful. Then, imagine your auric field shrinking so that it's tightly wrapped in a protective membrane of light around you, ensuring that you're not picking up anyone else's energy. See yourself walking through your day confident and unaffected by unwanted energy. Let go of the visualization when you're ready and feel yourself effortlessly melt into sleep.

#2: Make a Protective Bubble

Just like the practice above, try this practice the night before any kind of situation that might push you out of your center; you can also do this practice if you're accustomed to being in environments where the people around you push your buttons and boundaries. Set an intention to protect your energetic boundaries, which will naturally trickle over into your physical, time, and verbal boundaries. First, imagine pure-white light coming down from the cosmos and creating a bubble around you. This bubble can be as thick as you want; it deflects any negative energy that might come your way. Next, say the following affirmation out loud: "I'm now protected from all toxic, fear-based, negative energies around me. Anything that is not of the purest love and light is not allowed within my bubble. I am safe and loved." You can also use this technique during the day—perhaps before heading into a stressful workplace or family situation where other people's energy might affect you, or before heading to a family gathering where opinions and emotions are sure to run hot and strong.

#3: Take a Salt Bath

I love working with the elements to clear energy, and I especially appreciate the cleansing properties of water. Salt baths are wonderful for both physiological ailments and energetic clearing. We know that water, when mixed with sea salt or Epsom salt, can stimulate circulation, ease muscle cramps, alleviate stiff joints, soften achy limbs, and make us feel relaxed and rejuvenated.

Different kinds of salts are thought to have their own unique properties, for example, pink Himalayan salt is thought to purify our external environment. Dead Sea salt, which is packed with minerals, detoxifies the body. Epsom salt, which is composed of magnesium and sulfate, relieves stress. In many holistic practices, salt is believed to restore the flow and circulation of energy in the body. It is also often used as a protective and purifying ingredient that wards off negative energy and restores a sense of balance. Salt, which is abundant in ocean water, strengthens the immune system; studies have shown that people who swim in the ocean have a higher proportion of certain immune cells, like helper T cells, which can ward off infections. Protect your own energy, mind, and body, by taking a salt bath for at least three nights in a week.

You can do this by filling your tub with warm water, which will make it easier for the salt to dissolve. Choose your preferred form of salt (I like Epsom), and add at least a cup to the water. You may wish to add more if you're feeling especially depleted—which is a sign that your energetic boundaries have been trampled. A salt bath will restore and rejuvenate your energy, and wash away any negative influences. Let yourself soak for 20 to 30 minutes. As you soak, you may wish to incorporate any of the other practices in this chapter or listen to music that provides a sense of rejuvenation.

MORE RESOURCES AND FREE DOWNLOADS

Protect your energy with clear boundaries! Listen to the **Energy Protection Meditation Audio** to create strong boundaries that shield your energy from negativity. Listen here:

https://dothisbeforebed.com/resource

CHAPTER 8

CHANGE AND LIFE TRANSITIONS

Change is one of the greatest gifts that could possibly be given to us, and it's also one of the most difficult for us to accept. But, like nature, we are meant to evolve into the highest versions of ourselves. Just as the acorn holds the blueprint of the mighty oak tree within it, we carry the blueprint of our own infinite potential, waiting to be unlocked. This is why a life of predictable reliability is one of the worst things we could wish upon ourselves, because it's a recipe for stagnation. And yet, it is the picture that we're all taught to idealize from a young age.

It's completely fine to have a picture of how we would like our life to be. At the same time, that picture requires constant updates, because as our life experience shifts and our consciousness grows, we are going to stumble upon new discoveries within our inner and outer landscape—meaning that the visions we hold for our future will necessarily need to grow and change as well.

I have had so many students and clients remark, "If someone had told me that my life would look like this a year ago, I would have told them they were crazy!" That's because a lot of the people I work with often go through major shifts in a short period of time, such that they can barely recognize the person they were at the beginning of their journey. I always remind them that this is a great thing. It might feel destabilizing from time to time, but in truth, change is something we're already constantly doing, even when we don't recognize it.

That's why the greatest absurdity of all is the fear of change. From the moment you came out of your mother's womb, you have been in a state of continuous transformation. It's not actually unfamiliar to you, even though your reptilian brain (the oldest part of the brain that corresponds to unconscious behaviors of self-preservation) may cause you to see change as something that threatens your survival. All you have to do is remember that you've done it your entire life from day to day, month to month, year to year. There has always been at least one thing small or large that has shifted for you. You moved from elementary school to junior high to high school, and then to higher education and/or the workplace. You moved from home to home, city to city, country to country. And throughout your life, you've known so many different people: some were there only for a short season before falling away for good; others stayed longer; and some people who you assumed were gone forever suddenly reentered your life unexpectedly.

This is the nature of life experience. Certain rhythms may seem highly predictable, but others are entirely unpredictable. And it is this unpredictability that is such an exciting aspect of this great adventure called life. Throughout each of your inevitable transformations, you learned profound lessons that will be with you for the rest of your life.

Sometimes, even when they understand that the nature of life is change, people I work with express that they still feel daunted by the prospect of losing familiarity. A lot of them are making enormous emotional and spiritual shifts in their lives, and their fear often comes down to worrying that they'll be abandoned or rejected, or that change will take them too far away from their loved ones.

My student, Janice, was worried that her husband of many years, Dan, would ultimately lose interest in her and leave because she was pursuing a path of personal development that was so foreign to the life they had lived together up until this point. After a long history of working her way up the corporate ladder and doing everything society had expected of her, Janice experienced a series of synchronicities that took her in the direction of wanting to prioritize her spiritual path. That's when she found my energy healing school. Dan was bewildered about her decision, even though it had been a long time coming. I suggested that Janice speak to the fear of loss that was the elephant in the room, which seemed to be impacting both her and her husband in different ways. I suggested that she tell him, "Listen, I'm going to be doing this work on myself. I don't want you to think that by doing this, I'm leaving you behind. This is about me stepping into the best version of myself so that I can show up everywhere in my life, including our marriage, with the greatest commitment and joy."

What ended up happening, which is quite common for my students, is that Dan was actually appreciative of all the positive changes he saw happening in Janice's life. They actually made him more curious about the path of personal development. He began to take workshops with me, much to Janice's delight and surprise. Today, although their approaches are slightly different based on their individual personalities, both of them are pursuing a path of personal development that has enriched their lives for the better.

Basically, the lesson here is that you can stay exactly as you are and still end up losing the people in your life, key

regardless of whether you change or don't. The only variable that should make a difference is how *you* want your life to be. If you prioritize living at your highest vibration, the relationships you maintain will grow even stronger.

Of course, the fear of change isn't always something that is immediately at the top of everyone's mind. I've noticed other situations where people get the changes they asked for and it ends up feeling way too overwhelming. In fact, one of the most common things I see is that somebody does a significant amount of work to increase the efficacy of their manifestations. Then, something amazing happens. The promotion, job, business opportunity, relationship, or emotional breakthrough shows up. But the only problem is, the person who wanted it so badly discovers that they just can't receive it. They're not ready yet.

One of my other students, Harmony, decided that he wanted to manifest love. Somebody showed up in his life within a week, and it freaked him out! The good thing is that when we get cold feet after getting the changes we've asked for, we're being shown what we still need to work on. If we turn away from our desires because we feel overwhelmed by them, and we self-sabotage as a result, we can start to look more consciously at why. In Harmony's case, he figured out that he needed to work on self-love and actually believing that he deserved a fulfilling relationship, as he was still struggling with a great deal of guilt over his divorce, which happened over a decade ago and was one of the most painful experiences of his life.

I told Harmony, "What's going on right now is a good problem to have. You're manifesting what you want so much faster than you used to. But now it's time to work on receiving the good stuff. It's your old programming that's getting in the way of welcoming the beautiful changes that want to happen."

Gradually, with many of the practices in this book, Harmony was able to release the blocks that kept him from welcoming the positive changes that were occurring. Today, he is in a joyous relationship and has become more adept at welcoming his highest good.

So, we've looked at the *fear* of change, but what happens when you welcome change but nothing seems to be happening? Typically, when I encounter people who feel stuck in their lives and are at their wit's end because they've been waiting for transformation to manifest and have put in the work but aren't seeing any results, their "why" isn't strong enough.

When people I meet complain that nothing is happening, I often ask them, "Why do you want to change?" I end up getting a lot of confused answers and excuses.

Ultimately, your why has to be strong enough to move mountains. If your why is big enough, any resistance that you encounter along the way won't trip you up. For example, if you're looking to change your lifestyle by eating in a healthier way because you've convinced yourself that you "have to," this probably won't be a strong enough fuel to achieve and sustain change in the long run—as "should" and "have to" are seldom very good at helping us stay inspired. However, if you go to a doctor who tells you that you need to change immediately or your health will suffer demonstrably, it's likely that you'll have the fire under your feet that's necessary to kickstart you into a healthy lifestyle.

In order to initiate any kind of major transformation, discovering your "why" is a must. It's a matter of finding a compelling enough reason to do the things you say you want to do. It's usually not that people *want* to consciously stay stuck; it's more that they haven't discovered a fuel that is big or urgent enough to help them bypass their excuses and get to the treasure that's waiting for them on the other side.

(handwritten margin notes: "major keys!!", "key !!", "important")

Another situation I've encountered when people are not experiencing the changes that they wish for is that they're simply not aligned with the right time frame. For example, there are certain things we can do that will get us immediate results, while other things will take longer, no matter how much work we put in. A baby takes nine months to create—not much we can do about that. In contrast, baking a pizza in the oven might take only an hour or so.

Also, a lot of times, when people are experiencing what may seem to feel like nothing happening, it's because they are expecting it to look a certain way. It could be that, indeed, a lot of stuff is happening beneath the surface or in a not-so-obvious way. Of course, I've already mentioned that I'm a huge fan of speeding up the rate of change. It's possible to do this in certain situations, especially when it comes to welcoming love, abundance, joy, and other positive states of being. In this case, it's all about vibration. While certain changes that we wish to make are going to have their own timeline, we can absolutely experience the states we'd like to be in right now, as long as we're not overly rigid about the forms in which they arrive to us.

For example, perhaps you have the desire to lose a certain amount of weight within six months. There may be a number of reasons it doesn't happen for you. But if you choose to make a change in your vibration and mindset, perhaps deciding that you will treat your body with kindness and speak to yourself with the highest self-love, this may actually speed up your desired results—or you might realize that the change you wanted in the first place was a greater amount of self-love, and the secondary goal of losing weight doesn't matter much to you anymore. Overall, as we discussed in Chapter 5, fixating on achieving specific goals can blind you to the deeper changes you desire, which are often more about your vibration and mindset than anything else.

I want to emphasize that change can be an extremely joyful experience that moves us further along our path. But there are definitely times when change can make us feel bereft and distraught, as if we lost our spark and are no longer the person we used to be.

I've had a lot of students and clients come to me asking, "What's wrong with me? Am I broken? I used to be able to feel so much joy, and now I no longer do." Sometimes, these students come to me in the wake of a difficult experience, such as a divorce or the death of a loved one. I always tell them, "Instead of feeling bad about yourself, I want you to celebrate yourself. The reason the thing in the past no longer works now is that you are growing. That thing doesn't work for you anymore, so it's actually a sign of progress, a sign that you're getting called to the next level of your journey."

When we come to a point in our life when the things that used to work for us no longer work, or the person we used to be feels like a stranger to us now, this almost always means we are in the process of creating a world and a future that is aligned with the person we are evolving into. So, if things start falling apart in your life and the person you used to be and the things you used to associate with your identity begin to feel unfamiliar, it doesn't mean you're regressing. In fact, it usually means that you're progressing. Whereas before you may have been treading water, you are now in the process of swimming toward something new. It might feel uncomfortable and confusing, especially if the landscape is totally different from the one you were accustomed to. But please be assured that in times of destabilization, the universe is actually working for you, not against you. And nature is here to remind you that evolution is your destiny.

THE PRACTICES

#1: "What's My Why?"

If there's a change you're looking to bring into your life that you're having difficulty with, perhaps because you're afraid or you're just not seeing results as quickly as you would like to, take five minutes to ask yourself, "What is my why?"

Create a why that feels deeply compelling and inspiring. It should be the kind of why that would enable you to move mountains. Only *you* can determine what your why is. If you don't find yourself coming up with an answer that feels right, allow yourself to connect with the light of universal consciousness. Feel it coming into your body through the crown of your head, permeating your third eye, flowing all the way down your throat, then into your heart and your solar plexus, and down through your pelvic bowl, as well as your arms and legs, until your entire body is a conduit of this universal light. Imagine yourself falling asleep bathed in this all-clarifying light. Trust that the dreams you have and the messages that come to you in the middle of the night will give you insight into a why that is strong enough to effortlessly pull you forward on the path to change.

Do this exercise every night for a week, and don't be surprised if a huge epiphany lands in your lap! It's even possible that your epiphany might be the realization that you *don't* actually want the change you are asking for. This is also okay. Just be open to the wisdom that comes your way. If you have any vivid dreams, write them down and investigate the messages within them.

#2: "Life Is Happening for Me"

"major key"

If you're going through a particularly difficult transition in your life, please take time to gently say the mantra, "Life isn't happening to me; life is happening for me."

Entertain the idea that maybe whatever's happening to you is part of your major purpose and contribution in life. Perhaps you're dealing with this challenge because you're here to solve it or shed light on the issue. You can't come up with a solution if you think life is happening to you, because this attitude only leads to depression, resignation, anger, and defeat. You cannot effect meaningful change if you feel like a victim. Instead, change the lens through which you're looking at things.

Perhaps what is happening to you is helping you to become familiar with a pattern for the purpose of shifting or healing it. You're being given the experience for the purpose of empowerment rather than debilitation. As you breathe and repeat the mantra for a few minutes, come up with at least three different ways that you know life is happening for you. In my own past, when things were dire, sometimes the only kinds of examples I could come up with in the moment sounded like, "There's hot water in my pipes, so I can take a nice hot shower." No matter how big or small your examples are, shifting into gratitude and acknowledgment is a great way to ride the wave of change and to feel more empowered and purposeful in the process!

MORE RESOURCES AND FREE DOWNLOADS

Navigate life transitions with grace and ease! Get the **Life Transitions Meditation Audio** designed to help you move through changes with a calm and grounded energy. Listen now:

https://dothisbeforebed.com/resource

CHAPTER 9

COMMUNICATION AND CONNECTION

So many of my students and clients come to energy work to improve their lives. The number-one improvement they want to see is their ability to connect with others. They want to be more vulnerable and open—with a partner, their family members, their colleagues, and their community—but for some reason, that desire for connection keeps getting short-circuited by a plethora of issues. These might include small and major misunderstandings, difficulty communicating, the fear of being rejected, or the story that other people don't really like or love us. These days, loneliness is an epidemic, which exacerbates our capacity to communicate and connect. I meet so many people for whom connection feels difficult, and many of them sadly come to believe that it's impossible to have the kinds of vulnerable, loving, open, and connected relationships that all of us desire on some level. On top of all that, we are living in an increasingly polarized world where we are more likely to see other people as our enemies or our competitors, rather than our allies and collaborators. We are often taught to fear one another, rather than to recognize that we are all parts of <u>one unified whole</u>.

key

Most of us tend to blame our lack of satisfying connection on external circumstances, like the environment that we're in, or the level of consciousness in the people we're interacting with. However, the first key to having the kind of connection you desire is to start with yourself. What are you doing to engender honest, open communication? A lot of times, I recognize from people's stories (especially their language and unchecked assumptions!) that they're communicating with the people in their life from an anxious or triggered space.

For example, maybe someone walks into a conversation with you feeling angry or annoyed. All of us are energetic beings, so it's relatively easy to pick up on the fact that the person who's trying to engage with you is doing so from a triggered or emotionally cloudy space. Sometimes that can feel like they are tugging on your energy and they want something from you. This can be uncomfortable when you're the person on the receiving end because it precludes the possibility of reciprocity and mutuality. If someone is talking to you in order to get something from you or in order to fulfill some kind of selfish objective, how likely are you to be interested in what they have to say?

Now, most of the time when we are communicating from a triggered space, we don't necessarily know this is what we're doing. So, the next time you want to connect with somebody, notice what your reasons are and get very clear about what you wish to convey to them. Check your energy. Where are you coming from? What is your intention? Do you want to connect with this person in order to make them wrong? Are you trying to get something out of them? Are you trying to get something from them without necessarily being direct about what it is you want? Are you coming to them with a set of assumptions, or from a place of openness and curiosity?

key #1

Key
||

Simply getting clear about your intention can help you move beyond the many problems people may struggle with in the attempt to have the intimacy they want.

My student Brad complained about the fact that he never seemed to be able to talk to his girlfriend in a meaningful way when she came home after work.

"How does that actually look and feel?" I asked.

"Well, I talk to her when she comes home from work, and she just brushes me off because she says she's tired and wants to go do something else. Here I am, trying to connect with her. And here she is, basically telling me I don't matter," he responded, visibly frustrated.

"It sounds like you've made the assumption that you don't matter and you're now blaming her for that rather than authentically attempting to connect," I said. "Is it possible that this attitude is coming into your interactions with her, and that might have something to do with how she's receiving you?"

He thought about it. "I guess that maybe I do come on kind of strong and this is pushing her away."

I suggested to Brad that maybe he needed to clarify his reason for wanting to connect with his girlfriend. He realized that he was coming from a place of needing her to validate him, to show him that she cared. But in fact, this was actually serving to push her further away. She was usually tired after her long nursing shifts. Brad's energy felt simultaneously needy and resentful, and she didn't have the wherewithal to deal with him when he was like that.

Brad changed his tactics and decided that he would try to connect with his girlfriend by preparing a cup of tea for her and asking her about her day when she came home. He noticed that communicating in this way actually made her much more open to talking with him because she could see that he wasn't trying to get something from her, but was simply trying to be present with her.

A lack of clarity when it comes to our own desires for connection can sneakily sabotage our relationships with others because we might be saying that we want one thing, when in truth, our actions are conveying something else altogether. This is also why I advise people who wish to communicate with another person, especially when that communication might be a hard conversation, to give them a head's up by naming the reason they wish to talk. I'm sure most of us have had the nerve-racking experience of a boss or a partner saying, "Let's talk," without offering us an explanation. This kind of ambiguity can create a lot of unnecessary anxiety. Suddenly, a simple request can send someone into an emotional tailspin of worst-case scenarios.

key =

At the same time, while transparency is certainly valuable, there are situations in which it's not always the best path forward. Some people say, "Let me be honest with you," only to offer too much information and offload everything on their mind onto the other person, which can be overwhelming—especially when it includes things like accusations and judgments in the guise of truth-telling. It's important to balance out our truth with love. *Important!*

Again, clarity is key here. Are you giving someone a piece of your mind simply to clear your conscience, or are you attempting to create a bridge of greater understanding between you? Are you saying a lot of different things, or do you have a single message you'd like to impart? Often, when we have multiple messages in our communication, the other person cannot absorb 90 percent of it because they feel bombarded. My belief is that it's the responsibility of the person communicating to ensure that the message is being received. For example, if you're speaking French and the other person only speaks English, your message is not going to land because you are delivering it in the language *you* feel most comfortable with. It's your job to ensure that your message is being received the right way. How do you do this? First of all, put yourself in the other person's shoes. Empathy is a powerful skill to develop.

For a moment, imagine that you are not yourself. You are this other person. Instead of making assumptions, get really curious. Who is this person? How do they think? What is their general temperament? Are they loud and aggressive, or gentle and quiet? Imagine what it's like to be them. Check out their body language to determine if the timing for the conversation is right for them. Are they in the middle of an important task? Are they about to run out the door? Might they need to get something off their chest before you start talking? Are you pouring enough love into the situation? These are just some of the filters to run through as you're about to have a meaningful or difficult conversation with somebody.

If you tend to be someone who prefers to talk rather than listen, take a step back. I have noticed this tendency with my father, who is well meaning but often talks over other people in a rush to get his message out and to feel understood. The way forward, especially if you want to engender better communication and intimacy with other people, isn't to merely speak. In a lot of situations, especially ones in which there is already tension, it's unlikely that the other party is going to listen to someone who's doing all the talking. The way to get to a space of openness and connection is to listen first.

You might approach the other person with the desire to communicate what's on your mind, but begin by letting them speak first. How do they feel about entering the conversation in the first place? What are some of the assumptions and questions they have? You might wish to sit with that information and delay your original conversation. Whatever the case, don't go into your interaction with the goal of being heard, which will come across even if you act like you're listening. For example, you might be communicating with a defensive posture, your arms crossed over your chest. Nonverbal communication is about 93 percent of our communication altogether. Be sure to maintain an open, nondefensive posture and eye contact, which will indicate that you're actually listening. Most of all, listen in order to understand and empathize with the other person, not to respond or make a case against them. If you truly want connection and open communication, you must value the art of listening and making sure that there's a safe enough space for everyone to be heard.

major key!!

Finally, I often advise people who are about to go into a tense or difficult conversation and feel nervous about it to rehearse the experience by writing down exactly what they want to say. Contrary to popular opinion, I'm a big texter and e-mailer. There are many situations in which having a face-to-face conversation with another person isn't possible or even ideal. In such a case, it's important to be able to shift to another form of communication. Moreover, plenty of people grew up in an unsafe environment with lots of yelling, and they may find it difficult to express their truth in the moment. They might have a tendency to shut down or to get overly defensive and aggressive. This is not authentic communication, because it comes from a triggered and traumatic space in which they are usually stimulated by their past experiences rather than their present reality. In such cases, face-to-face contact only exacerbates the situation. It can feel safer and more authentic to write down what they have to say, either with the intention of speaking those words with someone face-to-face or sending them via e-mail or text.

I'm currently working with a very high-powered couple who routinely experience difficulties communicating with each other. When they attempt to talk matters through, they often end up being too wounded and triggered to have a productive conversation. They quickly realized that attempting to talk things through put them at cross-purposes, which is part of why they sought me out. I encouraged them to write down their thoughts, feelings, and concerns when they were not triggered or upset, so they could share them with each other from a more authentic space that promotes connection and empathy. This is a more conscious form of communication rather than the verbal diarrhea they were both accustomed to—and it has served them well over the last several months. Today, they report greater ease and even enthusiasm in having meaningful discussions.

Often, when we are triggered, we end up saying things we don't really mean. But the cat's already out of the bag, and it's too late to take back our words. Sadly, this can generate lasting damage. Our communication can serve to bolster a greater sense of trust and connection, or it can take us further away from intimacy. Thankfully, all of us can learn to be more thoughtful about shifting the ways in which we communicate when we connect with our deeper truth and authenticity, and when we consider the vibration that we would like to be in as we communicate with the people in our lives.

THE PRACTICES

#1: Communicating Your Truth

We can use bedtime to activate our courage when it comes to communicating our truth, especially when we know we need to have a difficult conversation. I have coached students and clients through everything from important discussions with family members and partners, to ways they can stand in their authenticity when having a conversation with a boss or walking into a high-stakes business discussion.

Take five minutes to focus on the area around your throat, which is known as the throat chakra. This is the seat of your authenticity and capacity to speak your truth. Often when we experience constriction in this area, it's because we are not being completely authentic in our communication with ourselves and others.

Feel a bright blue light from the cosmos entering the space of your throat, activating your courage and authenticity. As you do this, feel any inhibitions melt away and visualize yourself having the conversation you're about to step into. Feel the outpouring of connection and authenticity as you lovingly speak your truth. See the other person or people responding in ways that promote a win-win situation and create more intimacy and connection. Do your best to experience the support of that beautiful blue light and to feel in your body what it would be like to speak your truth from the highest possible place. Do this visualization as often as you need to, and watch your connections change.

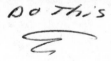

#2: Communicating on the Soul Level

The most powerful thing you can do when you experience negativity from others or difficulty communicating with specific people is to send them love. Take a few minutes at bedtime to imagine a beautiful, clarifying white light coming down from the heavens and enveloping the person in question with an abundance of love, light, and positivity. Next, imagine that light is wrapping you in the same love, light, and positivity. As this is happening, imagine that you are now able to be with this other person on the soul level. This is not someone who is dragging you down or causing anxiety or trepidation in your life. They are a pure soul, with their own wisdom and their own lessons to learn in this lifetime. Imagine that you are communicating with them from this place. You might have specific words you want to share (which you might never be able to share with their human self), or perhaps you simply radiate a sense of peace and care out to them.

Try doing this for at least three days, especially if you feel triggered by specific people in your life. Don't be surprised if your interactions with them change, or if the sense of difficulty is replaced by peace and clarity. One of my clients, Kevin, did this exercise when he was having issues with a neighbor who played loud music late into the night. Although Kevin wasn't able to have a productive conversation with his neighbor, this exercise helped heal Kevin's feelings of anger and frustration. Within a couple weeks, the neighbor stopped playing loud music and the enmity Kevin had for them melted away.

MORE RESOURCES AND FREE DOWNLOADS

Create open, honest communication! Listen to the **Heart-Centered Communication Meditation Audio** to help you connect with others from a place of love and clarity. Listen here:

https://dothisbeforebed.com/resource

CHAPTER 10

CREATIVITY AND INSPIRATION

Albert Einstein reportedly said, "The true sign of intelligence is not knowledge, but imagination." Imagination is also the gateway to thinking thoughts we've never thought before and dreaming dreams we've never dreamed. And if we can dream it, we can achieve it. However, the dream is only the beginning. If you have awesome ideas but don't actually do the work to bring them to fruition, you might be exercising the power of imagination, but this doesn't necessarily mean you're being creative.

Many might say that creativity is one of the things that sets humans apart from other animals, because it allows us to take what once existed only in the abstract world of thoughts and concepts and bring it to life in our material reality. This can require a lot of time and space (once known as daydreaming, which few people seem to have time for anymore!), but more often than not, it's about having the capacity to view your life through a different perspective. This might sound like fun and games, but it requires a sophisticated set of skills and the willingness to test our own imaginative boundaries. That is, instead of thinking about things the same way we've always thought about them, we start to examine new possibilities and consider perspectives that might be very different from our tried-and-true ones. We become curious about our inner and outer environment. We go outside our comfort zone and become more tolerant of ambiguity or unpredictability, which might mean that the idea we started out with—whether it's a book, a musical composition, or a business—goes through a few permutations.

A lot of my clients and students are incredibly creative people who sometimes experience blocks in their capacity to get into a state of possibility. Many of them are writers, artists, and entrepreneurs who were taught that creativity is impractical and frivolous, and that it's better to stick to enterprises that lead to predictable, measurable outcomes. But we miss out on life when we fail to prime the pump of our personal creativity. We might get stuck in our point of view, applying rigid methods to problems that are screaming for novel solutions. *Flow* - - -

One of the things I often do to teach my students and clients to activate their creativity and bust through blocks is to increase the amount of time they spend in flow. *Flow* is a term coined by psychologist Mihaly Csikszentmihalyi, who describes it as an almost trance-like state of complete absorption and effortless concentration. Everyone from surgeons, to writers, to endurance athletes, to students studying for an exam, is capable of entering a flow state—because all of us are innately creative, generative beings.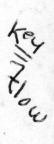

According to Csikszentmihalyi, when flow is maintained for long periods of time, it can lead to an almost spiritual state of ecstasy and clarity, where you know exactly what you want to do from one moment to the next, and solutions to problems "magically" arise. Our inhibitions and mental chatter melt away, and we lose our normal sense of time. We feel fully engaged, present, and connected to our superpowers. And even if we face some creative challenges, that's

major key

okay. In Csikszentmihalyi's words, "The best moments in our lives are not the passive, receptive, relaxing times . . . the best moments usually occur if a person's body or mind is stretched to its limits in a voluntary effort to accomplish something difficult and worthwhile."[*]

As someone who tends to thrive and be inspired within states that some might describe as "stressful," I couldn't agree more!

When I'm working with clients and students who are struggling with creative blocks or who want to feel more inspired, I often suggest taking on a practice that gets them into a state of flow. It might have nothing to do with what they'd like to accomplish, but it gets them out of the autopilot response of waking up, going to work, making lists, and following them—lather, rinse, repeat. Not exactly inspiring!

Often, the people I work with already have some sense of what gets them into flow: reading a book by a favorite author, listening or jamming out to a song, picking up an instrument, working out, playing with a pet, gardening, etc. Whatever the case, get a sense of the types of activities that make time disappear when you do them, and this will catalyze the flow state and a sense of clarity that is optimal when it comes to inviting the muses to break bread with you.

Sometimes, the setting we're in is also great cause for inspiration. Many people I know find that they are most creative when they're in nature, or when they're traveling. But the people you spend time with the most are also important. I surround myself with friends and peers with whom I can exchange ideas, which puts me into a state of creative flow. I'm also a firm believer in mastermind groups. This is a term that Napoleon Hill, the author of *Think and Grow Rich* coined to describe a group of peers who basically crowdsource

---

[*] Mihaly Csikszentmihalyi. *Flow: The Psychology of Optimal Experience.* New York: Harper & Row: 1990.

solutions to problems by talking through possibilities and offering input, feedback, and advice. I've been in a lot of business mastermind groups with other entrepreneurs, but such groups also exist for writers, artists, and other creative types who are seeking different perspectives.

A lot of times, for people who are in the midst of a huge project, such as writing a book or launching a business, it's not about how long you can stay "on." It really is about how long you can stay in flow, and how well you can create momentum. In physics, momentum is essentially mass in motion, which translates to energy. Basically, when you've achieved a certain focus and velocity, you're in motion and you're unstoppable. I mentor a lot of entrepreneurs who find it difficult to achieve this momentum, so I often suggest that, if they lack energy, they should try to focus on doing the easiest things first. This can create a sense of effortless accomplishment, which helps build momentum. Eventually, they'll be able to wake up and have the capacity to go after the hardest or most challenging things first, but the small wins are a great transition to get into that space.

When my mentees feel stuck, I remind them that getting back into flow is as simple as doing something they derive a lot of pleasure from, which can actually generate the kind of creative fuel that they can then redirect to their big projects. One of my mentees, Sara, received a huge energetic download about the website she was in the process of putting together for her holistic nutrition services—right in the middle of a women's soccer match! When that happened, I advised her to take a pause on everything else and act on her inspiration.

Essentially, an energetic download is a huge packet of information that can come to us instantaneously. We might receive it through our five physical senses, but more likely than not, we receive it through our inner senses (which you'll learn more about in Chapter 14). Energetic downloads usually seem to come out of the blue, and when we get them, it's like 100 light-bulb moments wrapped into 1. Usually, energetic downloads catapult us into new perspectives and realizations. That's because they come from a higher consciousness, meaning they enter not just our intellectual, conscious awareness but also our spiritual, subconscious awareness. We might feel a tingling sensation in our body, or some other kind of physical cue that helps us understand we're getting an energetic download.

Often, energetic downloads, which may seem to come to us via divine intervention or synchronicity, are the very things that take us to the next level of our creativity. If you get an energetic download, don't second-guess it. Stop what you're doing and put pen to paper, or start sketching out whatever has taken root in your imagination!

When I look back on my energetic-download moments, I recognize that they were essential "shortcuts" that trimmed down my work and efforts by what felt like decades. I've learned to take them seriously. Even if they come during an inconvenient moment, I put a pause on everything else and do what I can to ground that energy more deeply and take action.

If there's one thing I know is true, it's that incredible creative insights often come to us when we're not necessarily looking for them—for example, in the shower or right as we're falling asleep or waking up. Take advantage of your bedtime rituals to plant the seeds for remarkable inspiration!

THE PRACTICES

#1: High-Frequency Music

I have often found that energetic downloads are easier when listening to music that raises my vibration and gets me into a relaxed state. YouTube and Spotify both offer high-frequency music you can listen to. Simply typing in "high-vibration singing bowls" on either platform will lead you to pages of beautiful music that will steward you through the process of falling asleep. YouTube has a plethora of great videos, ranging from chakra cleanses with quartz bowls tuned to 432 Hz (a frequency that is believed to positively impact the body and mind because it connects us to a higher consciousness), to healing Tibetan singing bowls that help eliminate stress and emotional blockages. Winding down to these beautiful sounds will also prompt the parasympathetic nervous system response, the "rest and digest" state that heals your body and helps facilitate good sleep.

#2: Stimulate the Vagus Nerve with Guided Imagery and Visualization

As we fall asleep, we stimulate the body's parasympathetic nervous system response. The vagus nerve is an important part of the parasympathetic nervous system, and it has a huge impact on our mental health and mood. We stimulate the vagus nerve in a beneficial way when we utilize our imagination, engage in creative activity, and slow down. Here are three ways to stoke the fires of your imagination and stimulate your vagus nerve:

1. **Guided imagery** (using words, usually in the form of a meditation, to evoke imaginary scenarios that soothe the mind and body) can be a great way to spark creativity. You can find plenty of brief guided visualizations online, and I recommend you do these at least three nights in a row, which will prepare you for a night of creative sleep and dream!

2. **Visualizing outcomes** is another powerful way of delving into the fertile areas of your own imagination. After all, the subconscious mind doesn't know the difference between reality and imagination, which is why visualization is such a powerful technique to prime ourselves for our desired outcomes. Spend five minutes visualizing the best-case scenarios for your life or for a creative project you're working on. Take a few deep breaths and "see" your success in your mind's eye. But instead of attempting to control everything you see, notice if there are unexpected details that crop up. The hypnagogic state right before falling asleep is a powerful time to drop suggestions into the subconscious mind, but it's also a great way to get some unexpected downloads from the place where past, present, and future all coalesce!

3. **Make your own creative sanctuary.** This is a specific practice that will take five to ten minutes to do. Simply visualize or sense a color that connects you to a sense of your own creativity. For me, I love the color yellow-gold

because it reminds me of the life-giving energy
of the sun. Remember that creativity can come
in all kinds of varieties; you might be an artist,
gardener, wedding planner, or someone who's
just looking to inject more inspiration into
your life.

First, set an intention that you'll experience the color that brings about the greatest amount of creativity and inspiration. Then, imagine that white light is pouring down into your crown from the heavens. Next, imagine that this light is like a waterfall that is changing colors. Let yourself go through all the colors of the rainbow, perhaps even trying out other hues (magenta, electric blue, sunset orange, etc.). Notice which color fills you up with the most creative energy or excitement. Once you settle on the color, imagine a specific three-dimensional shape in that particular color forming around your body. You might wish to try a sphere, a pyramid, or something else.

Once you have your shape, say a brief affirmation: "My creativity is protected and blessed," sensing that you're in your very own temple of creativity. You can go to sleep with this protective, powerful energy all around you, or you may wish to continue visualizing all the magical places your creativity is bound to take you. Don't be surprised if you have vivid dreams (and don't forget to write them down).

Many of my clients and students who've done this simple practice have found themselves moving through creative blocks with surprising speed or giving more fuel to projects that are already in motion.

I felt like I was making my own special place for nourishing my creativity, my student Sage told me. Over time,

I'd come back to this place (my pyramid) and it would get bigger and bigger. I'd plant trees and gardens, add fountains, and do other things until it genuinely felt like I was somewhere real, somewhere I could go to and ask my higher self for guidance if I ever felt stuck. I'd just envision the space, get really quiet, ask my question, and wait for an answer to emerge.

I love Sage's idea of going to her creative sanctuary to find guidance over time. But please remember that the color and shape of your sanctuary might change, depending on what feels right to you. Be flexible and let yourself be surprised by what wants to flow through you.

#3: Creative Questions and Freewriting

Ask yourself, "What am I excited to learn? What am I excited to create? What are the breakthroughs I've had in the last few weeks that have shifted my perspective?" Then, give yourself 10–15 minutes to freewrite your responses. Freewriting is a mode of writing that has no structure in particular. You're not editing or censoring yourself as you write; you're just putting pen to paper (or finger to iPhone, although I personally prefer writing longhand) and letting your thoughts flow. When you focus on being excited and having breakthroughs, instead of feeling frustrated about creative blocks, your subconscious mind automatically receives the message that there's something to actually be excited about and that you are indeed having inspiring breakthroughs!

My student Sara, who had that amazing energetic-download moment, recently stumbled upon something she'd freewritten a couple weeks prior to that experience. She was astonished at some of the things she'd written, which directly related to her energetic download but that she'd totally forgotten about! Freewriting helps us access our creativity by opening a portal to insights we might not have in a more structured format. Do this exercise for at least a week—and don't be surprised if you end up having vivid dreams that further expand your sense of inspiration, or if you wake up with unexpected solutions to creative quandaries.

MORE RESOURCES AND FREE DOWNLOADS

Unlock your creative potential! Listen to the **Creative Visualization Meditation Audio** to access your inner inspiration and fuel your creativity. Listen here:

https://dothisbeforebed.com/resource

CHAPTER 11

FEAR AND ANXIETY

One of the biggest issues that my clients and students face is the sense of being held back by their own fear. A lot of times, they'll come to me because they feel blocked by an ever-present sense of fear that keeps them from moving into the peace, joy, and success they longed for. Sometimes, they'll ask me, "Oliver, can you help me break through my fear?"

I always explain to them that I do not necessarily see fear as a bad thing. After all, it's not that black and white. For example, if you're walking to the edge of a cliff and you feel fear, that's perfectly normal. It's an aspect of your biology and physiology that's there to serve you! Often, fear is appropriate because it allows us to discern between safety and danger. So, we definitely don't want to throw the baby out with the bathwater by getting rid of it altogether. Just as we keep fire alarms in buildings, fear is a very important alarm that allows us to process information from our surroundings and act accordingly.

Often, when it comes to the people I work with, fear is simply feedback about the things that are causing them pain, and it can guide them into further working to build the resources that help to alleviate this pain. On the other side of fear is something that is often beneficial to us.

For example, my student Jessica once said to me, "I know that I want to be successful with the work I do, but I'm afraid of humiliating myself and looking like a fool if I do it 'wrong.'"

As we dug into Jessica's fear, I learned that she was bullied a lot as a child and was routinely subjected to experiences of public humiliation that left deep, unhealed wounds. Even though she was very careful to present herself as a competent and confident person, there was a part of her that dreaded the possibility of failure because she couldn't bear the feelings of mortification that might arise from that.

Jessica and I worked together to explore some of the beliefs that had been generated from those painful experiences. As we unraveled her fear of humiliation (as well as her definitions of what constituted wrong vs. right, failure vs. success, and who had led her to form those beliefs), Jessica was able to move closer to her deeper desire, which was to be visible and to shine in her authentic passion. Of course, because she had had so many experiences that taught her to fear being visible, she now needed to learn how to reframe some of those fears and transmute that energy so that she could actually step into the things she most wanted.

I assured Jessica that she didn't have to fear fear. "Fear is a natural state that is an important part of the human experience," I said. And to that end, we don't have to get caught inside its vortex. But we also don't have to demonize it or turn it into our enemy. If we neutralize that difficult relationship with fear, to the point that it is no longer debilitating, we can get more curious about our inner states, which enables us to grow even more!

But what happens when you have anxiety, which is a much more difficult experience to unpack? Whereas fear can be defined as the body's response to a perceived threat, anxiety involves a sense of dread and worry about something that hasn't happened and might never happen. And while fear helps us to exercise discernment, anxiety creates a sense of unease that can result in long-term stress, restlessness, tension, and disconnection from ourselves and others.

I had another client, Eileen, who started to work with me in order to deconstruct her debilitating anxiety. It was so bad that she hadn't been to the grocery store by herself in close to 20 years. She was taking anti-anxiety medication, but it only helped to a certain extent. She still walked around with a sense of irritability and a feeling of impending panic most of the time. She had difficulty sleeping, as well as chronic stomach pain that came from literally making herself sick with dread.

As we deepened our work together, we realized that her anxiety (which, for her, seemed to have no discernible cause) was actually the result of extreme sensitivity to other people's energy. Eileen was actually a very gifted empath, and she learned to tap into this superpower while also being careful to protect herself with energetic shields. Every time she set foot outside her house, she felt a barrage of conflicting emotions and sometimes even messages that would flit through her mind in words or disconnected images. It was little wonder she felt so overwhelmed.

"I used to think it was just me," she explained. "But actually, I've always been a really sensitive person. It's just that I grew up in an environment where this was seen as strange, and something I couldn't talk about."

Eileen had never learned to channel her empathic talents. However, as she incorporated the foundational practices, as well as the practices in this chapter (as well as Chapters 7 and 14), her situation improved so dramatically that she was able to take trips to far-off locations on her own, without any problems.

Again, what we often perceive as anxiety is usually an issue of extreme sensitivity. I've also seen this with respect to people who are impacted by 5G, Wi-Fi, and electronics. Thankfully, although there are many environmental causes with respect to the kind of sensitivity that can lead to extreme anxiety, there are lots of things we can do to move through an anxious or fearful state.

I think of anxiety as being excess energy that we pick up from our external environment or from our old belief systems. If we start to see it as just energy, we can neutralize our relationship to it in such a way that it is no longer debilitating. When I was working with Eileen, I encouraged her to write out two lists. The first included her favorite ways of *releasing* excess energy—for example, dancing, working out, hanging out with pets, soaking up sunlight, or doing anything else that would allow her to naturally release tension, tightness, and dread from her body. The second list she made included her favorite ways of *channeling* excess energy—that is, redirecting it into other projects or goals. For her, some of these included making art, journaling, cooking a beautiful meal, helping someone who needs it, etc. She found that referring to these lists helped her develop some valuable go-to resources for dealing with anxiety, which would still come up every now and then. Eileen also discovered that intense healing could happen simply from getting eight hours of high-quality sleep during which her body could process the excess energy she'd received throughout the day, so that she would wake up feeling refreshed.

One last thing I emphasize to my clients and students is that many of us respond to our lives from a place of fear because it's all we have ever known. It's possible to transform this response over time by remembering that whatever has happened to us isn't what matters the most. It's our reaction to our experience that matters. For example, if you receive a bill from the IRS, it might result in feelings of fear and anxiety.

You might wish to avoid it because it brings up intense emotions around money and abundance, or lack thereof.

I used to experience fear and anxiety over unexpected bills myself, but when I learned that energy is just energy, it helped me to transmute my low-vibration thinking and shift into a state of gratitude. I was actually able to receive bills with a sense of appreciation! It allowed me to remember all the inner and outer resources I had, which helped me recognize that receiving the bill was actually an opportunity to shift into an abundance mentality. This led to a chain reaction of gratitude as I thought of all the wonderful things in my life that provided me with a sense of stability. When I began doing this, my experience naturally shifted. I no longer experienced anxiety around unexpected bills—or unexpected anything, for that matter. As I shifted into gratitude, more opportunities began flooding into my life.

A lot of times, fear is just a habit that's been handed down to us. I always find it's helpful to recognize that you are courageous by virtue of being on this planet. You're here, which means you've already lived through a lot, so allow yourself to feel grateful for your life experience and the wisdom that comes with it. Allow yourself to walk through fear so you can shine a flashlight on the dark shadows that other people may be shying away from, because that's all they've ever known how to do. Both gratitude and an acceptance of your natural courage are ways of owning your true power, while also empowering others to push through their fear and get to the gifts that await on the other side.

THE PRACTICES

#1: Release Fearful Thoughts

Use this quick exercise to release all stress and all negativity in your body if you are feeling the presence of debilitating fear and anxiety.

Set an intention by praying to your angels, higher self, or source consciousness: "Please help me remove and release all this fear and anxiety I'm holding on to in my body."

Next, take some deep breaths. I like the box breathing technique, which helps me to get into a state of deeper relaxation. Breathe in for four counts, hold your breath for four counts, then breathe out for four counts, and hold for four counts. Do this for at least five cycles.

Alternatively, another good technique is the 4-7-8 breathing technique, which is believed to reduce anxiety and increase our sense of inner confidence and well-being. You inhale for four seconds, hold your breath for seven seconds, and exhale for eight seconds. Do this for at least five cycles. (You may also wish to do five cycles of box breathing and five cycles of 4-7-8 breathing. Go with what intuitively feels best.)

Now, imagine white light coming down from the sky, filling your head. Visualize that as it filters through your body; your anxious energy is a cloud of smoke that gets pushed out of your body by the white light until it exits through your feet.

Because our fear and anxiety often come from old, outdated beliefs, as well as the influence of other people, you can now take time to cut the energetic cords attaching you to these things. As your body is filled with white light, imagine that there's a sword in one of your hands. It's a magical sword with the sole purpose of enabling you to cut toxic cords that keep you plugged into a state of unnecessary fear and anxiety. You don't have to know what or who you're attached to. Visualize that there are multiple invisible cords coming out of your body, connecting you to these influences. With your sword, cut those cords to the front and back of your body, from your head to your toes. Imagine that as you do this, you are cutting away the power of other influences that may have served to fill you with fear and anxiety. Imagine that you are throwing those cords up to the sky, to be transmuted into pure energy.

Now, imagine the white light that's already filling you is rushing into those places where you cut the cords, allowing you to feel healed and rejuvenated. Thank the light and fall asleep, bathed in its loving protection.

#2: Soak Up the Sun

Unlike some of the other exercises in this book, this particular exercise is ideally done at sunrise, or shortly after waking up. If you tend to wake up feeling anxious, it's likely that your bed has become a toxic dumping ground for excess energy. Take time to go outside and soak up the sunlight, as the sun is a powerful source of energy that can clear away anxious thoughts and feelings. The sun is also a known serotonin booster that creates a natural sense of calm and focus. When we go without sun exposure for long periods, our serotonin levels decrease, which can make us susceptible to bad moods. Spend five minutes soaking in the sun as you do gentle stretches or move your body. Moving your body physically is also a great way to release excess energy and, complemented by the uplifting power of the sun and the grounding energy of the earth, you'll be bound to feel an immediate shift. I recommend adding this to your daily routine, as long as the weather permits!

#3: Remove Negative Energy from Your Home

As you already know, your environment is everything, and sometimes the specter of fearful energy can leave an unfortunate residue in your home. Science can't yet explain why this is so, but we've all felt it. We've all been to places that feel "off" or that have "bad vibes," just as we've likely had the experience of being in places that calm us and bring out our very best. If the space we're in doesn't feel good, this may be contributing to excess fear and anxiety. This means we need to cleanse and clear the air. The following has been a wonderful practice for both me and my wife, Mandy, who is extremely empathic and sensitive.

First, find a stick of incense, a bundle of sage, or a piece of palo santo, all of which have been used in spiritual traditions for millennia to clear out negative energy. Before bedtime, walk through every room of your house to "smudge" the space. Smudging is a practice among many different groups of indigenous people that involves burning herbs to cleanse an environment and eradicate any negative energy.

As you do this, ask a higher power or whatever you believe in for assistance. I personally enjoy working with Archangel Michael, who is known as a formidable protector capable of eradicating any toxic energies that might be messing with our sense of tranquility. Speak your prayer or request out loud. For example, "Archangel Michael, source energy, higher self, higher power, please make my home a sanctuary that cannot be penetrated by any toxic, negative, fear-based energies."

As you move through each room, visualize the negative energy melting away and being replenished by an energy of love, peace, and serenity.

Finally, imagine that beings of light are protecting your entire home, standing as guardians around the property. Conversely, you can imagine that your home or property is shielded by a giant sphere of white light whose purpose is to keep any negative energy out of the house.

Thank any guardian spirits you summoned, and let yourself drift into a peaceful sleep.

MORE RESOURCES AND FREE DOWNLOADS

Release fear and anxiety before bed! Listen to the **Let Go of Anxiety Meditation Audio** to relax your mind and body, and experience deep inner peace. Listen here:

https://dothisbeforebed.com/resource

CHAPTER 12

HEALING GRIEF AND TRAUMA

One of the most difficult experiences we can go through in life is that of sitting with the pieces of our shattered life in the wake of trauma or intense loss. Many of my students come to me with the belief that they're broken in the wake of some kind of major loss: death, divorce, illness, or painful memories of abuse, assault, or moral injury—all of which can draw people onto the path of spirituality and personal development.

One of my clients, Matt, came to me after receiving a cancer prognosis that gave him only up to two years to live. Matt wasn't only grieving his mortality, which would mean leaving behind his beloved wife and young daughter. He was also in a state of grief over many of the things he believed had been left unfinished in his life. Matt was estranged from his parents after a turbulent and abusive childhood. He felt heartbroken that he would probably never get a chance to speak with them again. In a way, Matt was shell-shocked by the news of the few months he had left, but he was also softened by it. It helped him to recognize what he still felt he needed to work on.

I'll come back to Matt's story shortly, but I first want to emphasize that grief and trauma are not necessarily obvious experiences. Trauma experts talk about two different kinds of trauma: big T and small T. Whereas big T trauma usually refers to ongoing trauma, such as repeated abuse or intense experiences, including war and natural disaster, little T trauma is different. It might include things like emotional abuse, bullying, or the death of a loved one, but it doesn't usually involve extreme violence or injury, although it can still create a sense of distress and everyday wear and tear that adds up over time. Contrary to popular belief, big T trauma isn't any bigger or more grievous than little T trauma. We're all unique individuals who respond to adverse circumstances in different ways, so it's a good idea to be compassionate with ourselves, whatever our experiences of suffering might be.

As I reminded Matt, and as I like to say to all my clients and students, trauma can feel debilitating because it robs us of our sense of agency and essential goodness, but it isn't who we are at our core. Once we begin to do the inner work, we start to recognize that we are so much bigger than our trauma. But first, it's a good idea to understand trauma at its basis.

Dr. Peter Levine is the founder of Somatic Experiencing, a modality for helping people to loosen trauma in their bodies. Dr. Levine describes trauma as an experience of extreme fear in the face of helplessness. Our individual responses to trauma can vary a great deal, but they result in the same thing: a sense of suffering. When we undergo a traumatic experience and are unable to complete the fight, flight, or freeze response, the impact is that our body remains in a stuck place. It's almost as if some part of us gets frozen in time.

Thankfully, there are many things we can do to accelerate the process of healing and alleviate the sense of stuckness. A lot of times when I'm working with clients, I recognize that the painful experiences they went through aren't the problem. The problem is that they have never been able to fully process or express their trauma in some way. For example, when we have undergone a loss or anything that damages our sense of self, we must be able to grieve. In this way, something as simple as allowing our tears to flow and expressing intense emotions in the presence of a loving witness can take away so much of the heaviness that we associate with grief and trauma.

In my second session with Matt, he was able to cry for almost an hour straight, which was an incredible feat, given the fact that he'd told me he hadn't cried since he was a small child.

Matt also revealed that in his early adulthood, he had struggled with substance abuse, which didn't surprise me, as addiction is often the result of unprocessed trauma. It's our distorted way of offering ourselves comfort in the wake of a difficult experience that we haven't learned to process because we haven't been willing to fully feel our emotions. Indeed, fully feeling our emotions isn't the easiest thing to do if we're trying to avoid triggering memories of trauma. This is why working with a grief counselor or healing professional is extremely helpful. Overall, once we are able to process what happened to us, it becomes easier to release the effects of debilitating trauma and grief in our body.

But what if you've been through something in which someone else has wronged you? As I mentioned, Matt dealt with a difficult childhood in which both of his parents were abusive and neglectful. Some part of him really wanted to come to terms with his unhappy childhood before his own death. At the same time, he hadn't been in touch with his parents for so many years, and he felt that forgiving them wouldn't be genuine.

I gently explained to him that forgiveness is overrated. "You can absolutely move on without ever forgiving your parents if you don't choose to." I explained that instead of getting stuck in dogmatic thoughts about the necessity of forgiveness, he might want to frame the situation in a different way. Rather than thinking of it as "forgiveness," he could choose to simply release the anger and pain he was holding in his heart toward his parents, so that it no longer affected him.

I explained to him, "You might still have feelings of sadness and never forget what your parents did to you. But that memory doesn't have to be a toxic influence that riles you up and causes you to suffer."

Over the next few weeks, we worked with the idea of releasing the painful sensations that still gripped Matt when he thought about his past. In fact, it became easier for him to view his parents through the lens of compassion, because he had released the energy of abuse without forcing forgiveness.

Incredibly, when Matt's parents found out through his wife that he had been diagnosed with a terminal illness, they were able to put aside their differences and be there for Matt. Matt's father in particular was surprisingly supportive and even shared some previously untold stories about his own childhood, which had resulted in some of the choices he'd made in parenting Matt. As it turned out, Matt's paternal grandfather had been extremely abusive toward Matt's dad, who'd learned to toughen up and change his sensitive exterior to one that was virtually impenetrable. Unfortunately, this had filtered into his relationship with his wife and only son, Matt.

Matt's father tearfully shared all this with Matt, which led to another breakthrough: The difficulties Matt had experienced didn't start with him. A pattern of intergenerational trauma started to make itself evident. The men in Matt's lineage had struggled with abusive parenting and subsequent issues with addiction and health disorders. In learning that the pattern didn't start in his childhood, Matt was able to relinquish ownership over what had happened, which had essentially caused him to feel responsible for the abuse he'd grown up with. Matt's transparent interaction with his dad also enabled him to foster the belief that he could break the cycle and release the pain that had tormented his father and his father's father, and so on.

Incredibly, Matt found himself somatically releasing an enormous amount of trauma and processing his pain extremely quickly. As he told me about two months into our work together, "I find myself getting through difficult events and emotions super quickly, and processing through some of the biggest fears that have held me back in my life, such as fully expressing my love to the people around me."

Not surprisingly, Matt ended up not only defying his prognosis altogether, but all traces of his illness disappeared within several months of our work together; he has been healthy and happy ever since. Moreover, he has repaired his relationship with his parents, who are now enjoying being grandparents to Matt's beautiful daughter.

Matt's experience of healing his own trauma, as well as his illness, is proof that being aware of everything we've been through and processing it in a responsible and methodical way can help us break cycles of trauma that often hold entire families captive. Matt's incredible work has helped him recognize his own deep capacity for healing. Today, he is a gifted therapist who helps families who have experienced abuse and estrangement to come together to heal intergenerational wounds.

I see stories of powerful healing, like Matt's, on a daily basis, and it's a privilege to be a part of my clients' journeys. However, one thing I want to emphasize is that healing is not necessarily a linear process. And while it can absolutely take place at a quicker rate when we open ourselves up to all possibilities, there are certain losses that simply require the balm of time and self-compassion. For example, if we are in a grieving process that casts a shadow over everything else in our life, it's important to be in that process without bypassing or rushing through it, which only serves to prolong the healing process.

If you are dealing with acute grief right now, it's important to make self-care your utmost priority. You might need to sleep more or spend weeks binging Netflix shows and engaging in coping mechanisms that give you the space to process whatever you're going through in your own time. I usually suggest that people move toward feeling their feelings, but trying to step right into the storm when it seems like your world is falling apart is not advisable. It's okay to titrate your experiences of intensity so that you are moving in pace with your own capacity.

Matt, who now helps people move through intense grief, has told me that it often takes his clients time to recognize that their suffering has a purpose and meaning. First, they have to go through that difficult but necessary phase of the dark night of the soul in their own time while offering themselves plenty of self-care.

If we're grieving, we might not necessarily be doing it in the highest vibration possible. But even in these moments, it's good to be gentle with ourselves and sit with the reminder that this, too, shall pass.

THE PRACTICES

#1: Balance Grief with Joy

Love helps us to process grief in a healthier and faster way. If you're feeling intense grief in the wake of a trauma or loss, take five minutes at bedtime to replay the happiest moments you've ever felt—times when you felt the most loved or excited—almost as if you were watching them on a movie screen. If you've recently experienced the death or loss of a loved one, if it feels right to you, you might choose to recount positive memories associated with this person. If that feels too triggering, focus on other memories. Often, when we are in a state of grief, we unconsciously feel that allowing ourselves to be happy means we're not properly grieving or being loyal to the person we lost. This isn't true. Welcoming joy increases our capacity to be with difficult experiences. It allows us to welcome the bittersweetness of life, which includes all of its joys and sorrows. As you let the energy of love into your heart, you will experience a greater sense of balance and peace.

#2: Shake It Off

Many trauma therapists and specialists have noted that animals in the wild are often under duress but rarely experience long-lasting trauma—perhaps because they typically "shake it off" after coming face-to-face with danger and surviving it. Animals that survive a predator attack, for example, may involuntarily shake afterward, which releases a cocktail of adrenaline, cortisol, and other chemicals that help them to feel a sense of physical release. Humans, on the other hand, are taught not to have a physical response to trauma, but to breathe and calm down.

If you're feeling like you're in the throes of grief and trauma, which might not be the result of a single event but a series of experiences that have become frozen in your body, try shaking it off. Take five minutes to intuitively note where trauma may be stuck. You might feel it as tightness or tension in your throat, heart, or belly, or somewhere else in your body. It might also manifest as numbness or pain. Vigorously shake your arms and legs to release any "stuck" or "blocked" energy. You might imagine that there's a bug on your body that you're trying to remove without touching it. You might also want to try jumping up and down and releasing sounds in order to make this experience even more cathartic. Don't worry if you feel silly or self-conscious. The more you do this, the better you will feel.

#3: Transmute the Energy

One of the fastest and most powerful ways to release trauma you've been holding on to is by doing a fire ceremony. I worked with Matt on this process, which can be done at bedtime as many times as you need.

First, take a few minutes to write down the trauma that you want to release. You might include anything about the ways in which you've been hurt, including the people and situations associated with whatever you wish to release. In this way, the energy of your trauma is being released from your body and mind to the piece of paper you've written it on.

Next, burn the paper in a fire-safe container. Feel the fire burning through that trauma and transmuting and purifying the energy, so that you can go through your life feeling free and clear and unburdened from past experiences.

Next, write on a piece of paper what you'd like to replace the energy of the trauma with. For example, when Matt went through this process, he wrote, "I'd like to replace the energy

of my childhood trauma with a sense of joy, love, and gratitude for the connections I have with my wife and daughter."
Place that piece of paper that holds your intention on an altar
or under your pillow, trusting that you've made the space in
your life to draw this energy closer.

MORE RESOURCES AND FREE DOWNLOADS

Heal your heart from grief and trauma! Listen to the
Emotional Healing Meditation Audio to process
grief and release emotional pain in a safe, guided
practice. Listen here:

https://dothisbeforebed.com/resource

CHAPTER 13

HEALTH AND VITALITY

Everybody has the desire to feel good in their body, and health has always been a major issue for my clients and students, who often come to me for the first time when they're experiencing some kind of disruption in their physical, mental, emotional, and spiritual vitality. Although we have a tendency to split health into lots of different categories, all these are actually interconnected. Our body itself is a vehicle in the material world that facilitates both our physical and nonphysical experiences—but ultimately, our body is energy on an atomic and subatomic level. So, ultimately, health is an energetic imprint—the literal frequency and vibration of our energetic structures, including our physical and nonphysical (also known as "etheric" or "subtle") bodies.

I define health as a state of optimal well-being that promotes the unencumbered flow of energy through all our systems, including our body. Optimal well-being means that we experience what it is to thrive in these temporary bodies; it's not about remaining at baseline or stuck in a neutral place where we don't experience sickness but we're also not at our most vibrant. At the same time, optimal well-being doesn't mean everything's puppies and rainbows all the time or that we won't run into challenges. In fact, challenges can make us more robust. Think of how strength training helps us build endurance and muscle mass. In the same way, we can use our life challenges to actually increase our vitality, as well as the flow of energy we experience.

Unfortunately, most of us are not really taught how to do this. A lot of people I know struggle with many different aspects of their health. Many who come to me say, "Oliver, I'm so low energy and I don't know what to do"; or "I really hate the process of aging and what it's doing to my body"; or "I'm struggling with my weight, and I'm not feeling comfortable in my skin."

Unfortunately, such attitudes tend to focus on the external—including what other people think of us, and how we appear to the rest of the world. Throughout this, we might not be paying attention to the internal landscape of our habitual thoughts and emotions, which directly impact our overall energy and health.

I am not the kind of person who believes that health issues are exclusively caused by "negative thoughts." Indeed, they might stem from generational patterns, or the foods we eat, or the toxins we are exposed to, or emotional patterns we haven't come to terms with. I try to emphasize that the source and what caused it doesn't matter. We can work with whatever is present if we bring it all back to how we are using our energy.

I have a lot of clients who come to me with a sense of energy overload. They've absorbed negative energy from their environment, or they've taken on too many responsibilities and activities, which ultimately leads to their body shutting down. The body talks and it's quick to tell us, "No more!," especially if we're overdoing it and running on fumes.

I've also witnessed people who had a variety of energetic blocks that have impacted their physical bodies over time. For example, I've had students who are meant to shine—by speaking to audiences or sharing their work with the world in a more visible way. However, they were afraid of being seen and of fully expressing themselves. When this happens, it's not unusual for that particular energetic blockage to eventually manifest as an issue in the circulatory system and our ability to breathe. One of my students was struggling with asthma, which made it difficult for her to maintain the stamina required to do some of the work she was doing with large audiences.

I've also seen people develop issues in their throat chakra, sometimes with repeated occurrences of strep throat. The throat chakra is connected to our capacity to speak our mind and truth, so when I see issues with someone's throat, I generally sense that they have restricted their self-expression in some way.

Other times, I've encountered people who've been holding on to too much pain and trauma, and they're just not ready to release it, which can often manifest as literal heart problems. Other serious chronic conditions are often the result of experiencing a series of compounding hardships that can make us feel weak or disconnected from our bodies. Energetically, we're saying, "I don't want to be here!" This can end up plaguing us for years, by creating a domino effect of disempowering emotions that only serve to feed our overall illness and lower our vibration so that illness becomes more plausible.

Again, it all comes back to energy and frequency. In fact, health or lack of it can literally be measured. We can see the energetic frequency of a healthy liver is very different from that of an unhealthy liver. This measurable frequency can give us a lot of information about what is required in order for us to live optimally, with excellent health and a sense of our own vitality, versus in a state of attempting to merely keep our head above water.

We live in a society that tends to be focused on getting us to the bare minimum of health rather than teaching us how to be our very best. And overall, our healthcare system is focused on treating symptoms rather than the whole person. This can lead to all kinds of disruptions in the flow of our energy, because we're only looking at one tiny part of a very large territory.

The great thing is when we start to pay attention to our energy and to work with our health on an energetic level, the supposedly impossible can happen. You might remember my client Matt, from Chapter 12, who not only survived a seemingly incurable cancer diagnosis, but is now thriving. And once, I worked with a highly sensitive, empathic woman whose muscles degenerated over time after she'd soaked up the energy of others for too long. I taught her to work with setting boundaries, which you learned about in Chapter 7, and amplifying her psychic senses, which you'll learn more about in Chapter 14. After doing all this, she was able to fully recover her mobility.

When we pay attention to what's occurring on the subtle, non-obvious level, we can defy statistics and expand what lives inside the realm of the possible. After all, we are naturally self-healing beings who have the ability to experience even greater vitality than we've been accustomed to in the past!

Typically, when I'm working with someone who's looking to restore their health, I generally look for one of two things. First, when someone comes to me complaining of a lack of energy or vitality, it's usually because they're experiencing some kind of energetic drain, including the ones you learned about in Chapter 7 (drains associated with people, time, environments, etc.). This drain is literally creating leaks in that person's energy. When I come into the picture, I help students and clients become intentional about recognizing patterns in their lives that might be contributing to the drain. It's kind of like finding the leaky places in a plumbing system and plugging the hole so that no more water gets out.

The second reason people may not have as much vitality and energy as they would like is that they're not doing enough self-rejuvenation practices to really allow for an unencumbered flow of energy. A lot of times, they might be overgiving and they have a problem receiving, which creates an imbalance in their energy. Often, the trick to regaining their energy is allowing themselves to refuel by receiving rather than just constantly giving.

Sometimes, I have clients who feel disconnected from their bodies, which can also create a lot of health issues. When we feel disconnected from our bodies, we are not honoring the fact that we are spiritual beings existing in a physical dimension. We are meant to be here, and to experience joy and vitality in these bodies of flesh and bone. Unfortunately, lots of the media we take in might make us feel as if we don't have the "right" body. I have worked with a lot of people who've shared with me their insecurities related to body image. Often, this has to do with unquestioned belief systems and conditional ideas about love and acceptance.

For example, I once had a client, Maria, whose parents celebrated her only when she was at an ideal weight. Every time she gained weight, which happened a great deal throughout her adolescence and early adulthood, she, her parents, and other family members would make derisive comments. Over time, because Maria had come to expect this kind of behavior from her own family, she unconsciously gravitated toward partners who would constantly make snide remarks about her weight. Although this was painful and dysfunctional, on some level, it felt familiar, like "home."

When Maria and I worked together, we discovered that her fear of losing love and connection had resulted in a sense of self-abandonment. She hated her body, which she had not been happy with for years. We worked a great deal with practices that would enable her to fortify her self-love muscle and stop abandoning herself by letting the people in her life put her down. Maria came to understand and dismantle the patterns beneath her behaviors. As our work continued, we rewired many of her limiting beliefs; she also learned to speak up and voice her feelings when she received cruel, inconsiderate comments from others about her weight.

Something else Maria and I worked on together was addressing her underlying craving for sweets. Whenever she experienced a craving, I suggested that she ask herself, "Why am I craving these foods energetically?" She was able to recognize that sweet foods were a substitute for the sweetness of genuine love and care. It was really important for Maria to recognize that her guilt and shame about her cravings was not getting her the solutions she wanted. Instead of beating herself up over this, she learned to become more discerning about the triggers that caused these cravings. I showed her how she could stay inside her body when those triggers came up and get into a habit of compassionately dialoguing with her inner child, who was feeling unsafe and looking for an outlet. We talked about other ways Maria could find the sweetness she was looking for.

Because she understood on an energetic level what she was needing, she had the opportunity to expand beyond her conditioned reactions and to do things differently. However, the judgments had to stop. Instead, she needed to become curious about what her cravings meant, and to love herself throughout her experience.

Maria found a sense of emotional sweetness in the volunteer work she did with children with special needs. This was such a huge source of satisfaction that Maria ended up going back to school to become a special education teacher. Incredibly, throughout that period, the weight she had struggled to lose ultimately came off. As she discovered a sense of purpose that renewed her energy and infused her with confidence, she no longer needed to resort to sweets. Also, around this time, Maria met another passionate teacher who celebrated her true beauty, which is about so much more than the way she looks.

Changing our mindset can transform our health, but what happens when you're faced with a serious illness that makes you feel like the rug was pulled out from under you? My experience is that many people who contract a serious illness feel they've "failed" themselves by getting sick. I've even met people who beat themselves up for not being more positive, or for letting in too much negative energy. But again, judgment is not particularly helpful.

We don't have to see our illness as a lifelong sentence, but rather as a wake-up call: a soul lesson that we came here to learn. Unfortunately, too many people view themselves as only their physical body, rather than an infinite soul, which can end up making them feel discouraged, depressed, and resigned to their diagnosis.

If you're experiencing an illness, I suggest joining communities of people who have healed their illness. Devote your life to being in environments with those who have significantly rewired their beliefs about health. You don't have to go by worst-case scenarios and limited perspectives about what your diagnosis means and where it's inevitably going to take you. If you're thinking, "I have a disease and this is the end," that's a sign that it's time to expose yourself to something bigger. This bigger perspective should involve the books you read, the podcasts you listen to, and the communities you're a part of. If you're focused on healing and purpose, your entire vibration will change and you will definitely experience healing. It might not look the way you think it should, but you will definitely raise your vibration and begin to feel restored to a greater energetic flow and more vitality, as well as inspiration and positivity—all of which make life so much more pleasurable!

THE PRACTICES

#1: Love Your Body

The Taoist teacher Mantak Chia revolutionized an amazing process he calls the "inner smile," which helps us to detox from negative emotions and feelings about ourselves and others. The thing that makes this technique so powerful is that it all begins with us and how we feel about ourselves. This process can take something like poor body image, or a negative perception of ourselves, and turn it into healing energy almost instantly. That's because the inner smile helps us cultivate a sense of gratitude toward our body for being the vehicle that moves us through life. Take about five minutes to go through this process, and feel free to gently place your hands over each body part as you feel the sensations and emotions that are present there.

Silently stating a specific intention, like: "I am available for greater health and vitality in my body [you can also name a specific body part, especially if you're having health issues associated with that part]," or, "I am opening up to my unique beauty," or, "I am connecting with my highest self, in order to feel more nourished, vibrant, and energized."

Place your tongue behind your teeth (according to the Taoists, this allows energy to circulate more easily through the body). Close your eyes and breathe deeply, breathing in for four counts, holding for four counts, then exhaling for four counts, and holding for four more counts. Do this a few times until you feel clear and relaxed.

As you focus on your third eye, let your face completely relax. Think of something that brings you a simple sense of joy. Allow yourself to gently smile. Let the smile begin at your eyes and then move down through your entire face. Allow the smile to be genuine.

Feel the energy of your smile flowing down through your body, softening your organs and filling you with light. It's like you are blessing each body part with an inner smile.

You may wish to say aloud, "Thank you," to specific organs and body parts as the inner smile flows down your body. For example, you might thank your throat for offering you the capacity for self-expression and allowing your voice to be heard. You can thank your heart for being the energetic center that allows you to radiate and express love, but also for pumping blood throughout your entire body. You can thank your lungs (which hold and release grief and depression, according to traditional Chinese medicine) for oxygenating your beautiful body. Allow yourself to be creative. You might even choose to thank your skeleton for giving you a sense of structure that helps you to move through the world.

Don't be surprised if you feel resistance, especially when it comes to parts of your body that you might feel ambivalent about or where you've been experiencing health issues. Don't worry if this is the case, but find something to appreciate about this body part, even if it's a neutral or aspirational statement, like, "Belly, thanks for helping me to cultivate deeper self-love," or, "Gut, thanks for breaking down the foods I eat and sending nutrients to the rest of my body."

If any strong emotions come, let them be there. This, too, is your body's way of communicating important information to you. Feel the gentle energy of your inner smile flowing throughout your body.

When you are complete, end your practice by spiraling energy around your navel. Men can place their palms left over right and imagine they are spiraling the energy clockwise 36 times; women can place their palms right over left and spiral that energy counterclockwise 36 times. Then, you'll reverse direction and spiral the energy 24 times. According to Taoist medicine, this keeps the energy stored in your navel, which means you'll avoid excess heat and energy in other parts of the body.

#2: Scoop Out the Energy Blocks

This is a powerful technique for quickly releasing any energy blocks you have in your body and also preparing you for a restful, restorative sleep. If you've ever experienced chronic pain, or even emotional suffering, all this gets stored in different areas of your body, which can hold you back and even lead to illness, which is why you have to be able to release them. Here's one way you can do that.

Let's say you're experiencing pain or low energy. Set the intention that a higher power is here, and it's going to remove all energetic blocks that keep you from feeling healthy. Imagine that a white light is coming down from the cosmos and filling your entire body. The white light is directing your attention to the places in your body where you need to pull out any blockages or kinks in the energetic hose—these might be places that feel tight, achy, dull, or even numb. Pay attention and let your intuition guide you.

Let's say you feel tightness in your heart. With your hands, make a motion as if you're scooping out any areas where there might be excess energy or any kind of blockage. You can throw it down to the ground or up to the sky to be released. Scan your body for areas that feel tight, achy, dull, or numb. Also, remember that whatever energy you take out, you have to replace. When you're done scooping out the energy you don't want or need, imagine that even more white light is coming down from the cosmos and filling your body, replacing any pain or toxicity that was there, rejuvenating you, and bringing you back to full health.

Do this exercise for five to ten minutes, or as long as you need to, whenever you are feeling blocked or in a less-than-ideal state of health, and watch your whole life change.

MORE RESOURCES AND FREE DOWNLOADS

Boost your physical energy and vitality! Listen to the **Body Healing Meditation Audio** to restore and strengthen your physical health and well-being. Listen here:

https://dothisbeforebed.com/resource

CHAPTER 14

INTUITION, PSYCHIC SENSES, AND WHAT IT MEANS TO BE AN EMPATH

We live in an exciting time, in which so many people are beginning to open up to their intuitive senses. We're starting to delve into the reality that the material world is only one aspect of existence. Many of my students and clients are budding energy healers and recovering materialists who are learning that their intuition is one of their greatest superpowers—and that the "unseen" realms are beautiful places to navigate. Culturally, we've made a lot of strides around these recognitions, but intuition isn't given the pride of place that it deserves in our society—even though the greatest and most inspiring teachers, leaders, scientists, innovators, and artists usually admit to relying on their intuition and psychic senses for the best results in their work and personal lives.

Because this chapter is about intuition, psychic senses, and what it means to be an empath (three subjects my students and clients take endless interest in), I want to break down what each of these concepts means.

We all have an intuition or a sixth sense, which can be defined as a feeling, usually in the area of our gut or heart, that tells us things we might not have otherwise known. Many scientists have theorized that intuition is just the result of all our unfiltered information, including what lives in the subconscious mind. So, it's not as woo-woo as we think it might be. In fact, neuroscientists have suggested that intuition is something that operates throughout multiple channels in the brain, particularly in the right hemisphere, the hippocampus (the part of the brain that regulates memory, learning, and emotion) as well as the gut (which is sometimes known as the enteric brain and consists of over 100 million nerve cells inside the gastrointestinal tract).

And then, we have our psychic senses. In truth, the only difference I've noticed between intuition and our psychic senses is that people who have honed their psychic senses have spent a lot of time paying attention to and developing their intuition. All of us have access to our intuition, and when we give it the importance it deserves, we cultivate psychic skills that might seem completely unexplainable—such as the ability to channel messages from other life-forms, communicate through telepathy, or even "see" the future." Although parapsychology (the study of psychic phenomena and paranormal claims) is still considered a pseudoscience, there's plenty of credible evidence (particularly from government experiments into matters like remote viewing, or the ability to "see" something that's happening at a far distance) indicating that our abilities far surpass what we know them to be. Personally, I'm greatly looking forward to the day when science is able to lucidly explain exactly how the psychic senses work!

And finally, we come to empathic skills. You're probably familiar with the idea of empaths, who have a high level of intuition that allows them to pick up cues from their environment, as well as from other people or animals. The only problem with being an empath, as many people have discovered, is that having such an acute sensitivity to others can be extremely depleting. Because empaths, who are thought to comprise about 2 percent of the general population, tend to be so perceptive and sensitive compared to most people, they can end up taking on other people's suffering and emotions without even realizing it. Many of the people who come to me as clients or students are earnestly in search of skills to work with their intuition, hone their psychic senses, and develop their empathic superpowers without getting burned out.

Generally, I find that empaths have to go through three stages in order to ensure that their natural superpower is working *for* them rather than *against* them. The first stage that an empath usually experiences is feeling extremely sensitive when they go to a crowded place, such as a mall or an airport. They feel overwhelmed, and they just want to get out of there. Any kind of overstimulation or exposure to people who may be operating at a low vibration affects an empath and throws them off. They could end up feeling this as tension, fatigue, anxiety, or even illness. Fear and anxiety are not uncommon among empaths, such as my client Eileen, whose story I shared in Chapter 11.

The next stage an empath goes through is that of neutrality. The more someone works on raising their vibration and doing the necessary healing to get to a place of balance, the more they actually start to increase their capacity to deal with negativity and intense stimulation, to the point where it just doesn't affect them as much as it used to.

The final stage is empowerment, which I attempt to share with all the people I work with.

Empowerment comes when we realize that if others can affect us negatively, the opposite is also true. Our energy has the power to uplift others. We can shine the light of our inner truth quite brightly, and this ability comes from a place of knowing exactly who we are and embracing our power and brilliance. When we walk in this vibration, we can't help but positively affect other people who are also intuitively feeling and being impacted by our vibe. We change the people around us, and we even start to benefit the world and the universe because we have come to own our true nature. We recognize that we are empaths who are sensitive to other people's energies. But while we can be affected, the light within us is a solution to the darkness that might exist around us. We see that our gift means we can be a force for change and healing on this planet.

This is extremely significant. So many of my clients and students misunderstand their incredible gifts and just want to be "normal." I once had a student, Richard, who felt that the people around him were always upset with him. He was living in an environment where others routinely became angry and triggered by the things he said and did, even if they were not at all inflammatory. Richard was a kind, mild-mannered person, so he couldn't understand what was happening. It got so bad that it became difficult for him to speak his truth and stand in his power, because he didn't want to rub people the wrong way. The reality, as I explained to him, is that he was a powerful mirror for other people. A lot of times, empaths reflect to others the very things they need to confront in order to heal.

Richard had the experience of people going from a level zero to a level ten and getting riled up while having simple conversations with him. I explained to him that he could work to be neutral in the face of strong reactions. "What's happening isn't good or bad," I said. "They're triggered because they see that they need to heal something that's coming up. And what you're doing is simply mirroring to them something that, hopefully, they'll be able to look at clearly one day so they can recognize their patterns and respond to the feedback in a productive manner."

When Richard finally got that one of his superpowers was his capacity to act as this radiant, clear mirror for others, sometimes without even saying or doing anything, it became easier for him to fully accept his empathic gifts.

Again, there's nothing wrong with being a mirror. In fact, those who are brave enough to stand in the light and mirror back to others the painful things they don't want to look at or that they don't want others to see are bringing enormous awareness to situations that are begging for healing attention. So, if this is something you can relate to, I urge you to own what it means to be a mirror. Again, this is not about intentionally riling other people up or treating them in a callous or unkind way. It's about noticing the impact your presence might have on people and recognizing that even if they react to you negatively, that doesn't necessarily mean you're doing something wrong. In fact, being a mirror is an extremely powerful purpose to have.

Aside from opening up to your empathic skills and redirecting them in ways that serve you, there are other things to notice that can help you hone your intuition and psychic senses. For example, perhaps there are times when you just *know* about things that are happening without knowing how you know. You might read someone's mind. You might start to see recurring signs, such as angel numbers: 1111, 2222, 3333, 4444, and so on. Often, when we see these numbers, they're pointing to some kind of deeper spiritual awakening we might be undergoing; they're also strongly associated with the opening of our psychic senses.

You might experience synchronistic occurrences. Perhaps you think about somebody for no apparent reason, and then they end up calling or texting you. In truth, stuff like this happens to many people on a regular basis. But because we're not paying attention to the signs and synchronicities, we might not realize that our intuitive and psychic senses are opening up in ways that could truly serve us.

I also strongly advise my students and clients to pay attention to that inexplicable feeling in their gut that might open up with respect to a particular person or situation. Our gut feelings are our guardian angels. If you have a strong gut feeling about a situation in your life, it means you are receiving a sign—which you might interpret as being from your guardian angel, your guide, or just your higher intuitive senses.

Of course, we all receive these insights in different ways, so I want to outline the eight psychic senses, also known as the *clair* (meaning "clear" or "bright") senses. The clair senses can be associated with both mundane life events (like knowing what your partner is thinking) and more esoteric matters (such as contacting the spirit of a dead relative). As you read over each of these, take note of the ones that feel familiar and the ones that feel unfamiliar.

Claircognizance: This psychic sense is connected to the gut feeling that comes when you know something but you don't know how you know, and you don't have any specific information to back it up—although that information often comes later down the road and corroborates what you knew to be true.

Clairvoyance: With this sense, you can see things in your mind's eye, or through clear visions or vivid dreams. These things might relate to future occurrences that haven't yet come to pass, or even past-life memories, as well as more mundane insights—such as having a vision of someone you know going about their day.

Clairaudience: This clair sense is connected to your auditory abilities. You might hear things in your head in the form of words, sounds, or even a ringing in your ears, which is typically summoning you to slow down and pay attention.

Clairempathy: With this psychic sense, you can tune in to other people's feelings and emotions as strongly as if they were your own. Again, until you develop a sense of neutrality and empowerment, it might be difficult to differentiate other people's thoughts, feelings, and emotions from your own.

Clairsentience: With this psychic sense, you can receive messages about other people or situations that you feel as palpable sensations in your body. For example, I have sensed illness or injury in other people through a gut sensation in my own body that is too strong and too real for me to ignore.

Clairtangency: When you have this psychic sense, you can touch an object, such as a book or an item of clothing, and receive powerful information that may come as a download of insights or just a gut feeling. Whatever you sense could be connected to the history of the object, as well as the people and places associated with that object.

Clairalience: This is a less talked-about clair sense, but it essentially refers to the ability to smell things that exist in the energetic realm. For example, my grandmother had a favorite perfume she loved to wear. During every anniversary of her passing, I smelled that perfume clearly, which is how I knew she was communicating with me and simply making her presence known.

Clairaugustance: This psychic sense is also somewhat rare and involves tasting things in the energetic world that might be associated with specific people or circumstances.

The eight clairs are a really great way to gauge your favored methods of receiving intuitive insights and information from the energetic world. It's possible to work with one or all these in greater depth, but it's especially powerful to pay attention to the ways in which energetic information wants to come through to you, and how and where it feels most natural. Just remember that anybody can develop their psychic senses, but working with them successfully requires cultivating an intentional practice of listening to your intuition (which we all have, although some of us may have forgotten) and fully accepting and honoring your empathic superpowers if you have them.

THE PRACTICES

#1: Open Your Third Eye

You can also do this exercise during the day, when there's sunlight, because the sun is an extremely powerful energy source that can be used to clear any blocks to intuitive/psychic/empathic insight. At bedtime, I find it effective to do this exercise beneath moonlight, which is a powerful symbol for intuition and the mysteries that exist beyond our five senses. You can also choose to imagine that the sun or moon is shining down upon you. Whatever the case, feel the energy of either the sun or moon filling up your outstretched fingers. When your fingers are filled with that luminous, powerful light, place them over your third eye and lightly massage. As you're massaging, say to yourself, "I am now ready to open my third eye, the seat of my mystical vision, for the highest good of all. I am ready, I am protected, and I am safe." Do this for at least a minute, three nights in a row.

#2: Sri Yantra Activation

The Sri Yantra is a powerful symbol in the Vedic tradition, composed of nine interlocking triangles. It has a number of different meanings for devout Hindus and lovers of sacred geometry, but many interpret it as being the symbol of divine union between the feminine and masculine aspects within us. As a sacred geometric pattern, it infuses us with positive, balancing energy. It also works to raise our vibration so that our chakras are operating at the most optimal capacity, which means we can receive information through our psychic senses more easily.

Simply gaze upon the image below, which will enable you to open up your psychic senses. You can do this for one to two minutes while saying, "Clear, clear, clear. Activate, activate, activate. Open, open, open," while you imagine your third eye filling up with the positive energy coming out of the Sri Yantra.

#3: Choose Your Clair

Choose one of the following clair senses and work with the suggestion connected to that sense for at least seven nights in a row, and I guarantee that you'll begin to experience signs, symbols, and synchronicities that you just can't ignore.

Strengthen Your Claircognizance: Working with this psychic sense will help you to trust your instincts more readily. Take a few deep breaths, clearing your mind of any thoughts, worries, or concerns to the best of your ability. Write down three questions about things you don't have the answers to and little information about. Read a question and notice the first answer that pops into your mind; write that answer down. It's helpful if your questions are associated with things you will have information about in the near future. For example, a simple question to pose might be: "What color will my co-worker be wearing when I see them in the morning?" Have fun with this process and don't take it too seriously!

Strengthen Your Clairsentience: Breathe into that place in your body that you most associate with your intuition. It could be your gut or your heart, which are fairly typical places for people to say their intuition resides. Ask a question about something in your life. Rather than expecting a straightforward answer, notice the subtle sensations in that area of your body. Feel into what these sensations might be telling you about the question you just asked. For example, I might ask a question like: "Where should I be putting my attention for the next month with respect to my business?" Perhaps in asking this question, I feel a sense of spaciousness and excitement in my gut, which I associate with gleeful anticipation. As I sit with that feeling a little longer, maybe I realize that it's allowing me to feel a greater sense of possibility—which could be telling me it's time to launch a new project or program.

Strengthen Your Clairvoyance: You can work with both the first and second practices in this chapter, since both of those activate the third eye, which is associated with clairvoyance. Another way to develop your clairvoyance is to spend some time visually examining the objects and details in your bedroom. Create a mental snapshot of a particular object—maybe a painting or a book on your nightstand. Once you do that, close your eyes and attempt to recreate that object in detail in your mind's eye. This one can take a lot of practice, so go easy on yourself and start small at first, perhaps only doing this for one to three minutes with a very simple object for a few nights before moving on to more complex mental images, such as all the details in one specific corner of your bedroom.

Strengthen Your Clairaudience: One exercise I enjoy is spending time listening to all the things that are in my environment, differentiating between sounds that are loud and ones that are much fainter, as well as sounds that are close compared to ones that are very far away. I once had a client who did this exercise and later told me that, over time, she felt she could hear the subtle buzz of the universe.

Strengthen Your Clairempathy: For this one, I suggest imagining that a large bubble of bright white light is enveloping you in a protective cocoon of positive energy. You can simply breathe this bubble into being, allowing your body to relax as you breathe. Feel how the bubble keeps out negative energy. After you do this, imagine somebody you care about and allow yourself to sense into the kind of experience they might be having in the moment. As you do this, ensure that they do not enter your bubble of protection. In fact, you can imagine them in their own protective bubble. Remember, clairempathy can be a tough one if you haven't already practiced creating good boundaries (in which case, I suggest you check out Chapter 7). Working with the protective bubbles will help you begin to do that.

Strengthen Your Clairtangency: Hold an object in your environment, such as a rock or a pen. Close your eyes and breathe deeply, noticing any insights that naturally arise, such as sounds, visions, memories, or even just a gut feeling.

Strengthen Your Clairaugustance: You can experiment with imagining different tastes on your tongue—for example, a salty flavor, like that of a potato chip; a sour one, like that of a lemon; and a sweet one, like that of a crisp apple. Often, when I have clients do this exercise, they feel their mouth begin to water as the taste becomes more and more tangible.

Strengthen Your Clairalience: Think of a scent you love that isn't lingering in the space you're in. The more distinctive the scent, the better. Focus on smelling this scent, until it feels real to you.

Keep in mind that these exercises take time and practice, so if you're keen on building up your psychic senses, be diligent and don't get discouraged if nothing happens at first. Even if you're only doing one of these practices for a couple minutes each night, your psychic senses will evolve over time if you're consistent and persistent!

OLIVER NIÑO

MORE RESOURCES AND FREE DOWNLOADS

Sharpen your intuition and psychic abilities! Listen to the **Intuition Activation Meditation Audio** to deepen your connection to your inner knowing. Listen here:

https://dothisbeforebed.com/resource

CHAPTER 15

LOVE AND RELATIONSHIPS

One of the most common reasons people find themselves interested in spiritual or energetic work is that they're looking for love and connection. We all innately understand that love is one of our fundamental states of being, and that when we have it, we thrive. That doesn't mean that life becomes magically perfect, but it does mean that we are strengthened by the positive bonds that we choose to forge with others. These bonds ideally help us to step into the best versions of ourselves, and to unlock our potential in an environment of the utmost care and support. We also get to be fully ourselves, and to experience what it's like to be mirrored by another person who deeply knows and sees us. It's little wonder that love, especially romantic love, is viewed as one of the most sacred experiences we can have.

Unfortunately, "love" is also at the root of so much wounding, and we may encounter a lot of distortions with respect to love, in everything from popular music to our own childhood memories. Many of us have experienced pain and trauma that arise from our early encounters with love, and we may find ourselves reenacting patterns of abandonment, rejection, neglect, or obsession and control—all of which we might even mistake for love.

During workshops and sessions, a lot of my students and clients go through a major revolution in self-love that enables them to recognize their patterns and break cycles of neglect and settling for breadcrumbs. One of my students, Alana, went through this revolution in her on-again, off-again relationship with her boyfriend. They had been together for 12 years when she came to one of my workshops, and she was at her wit's end. Alana had a strong desire for marriage and family, but her boyfriend couldn't commit. After about a week of doing some energetic clearing work, Alana realized that her definition of love had mostly arisen from a dysfunctional family environment in which she was not encouraged to have healthy boundaries.

Alana had a huge epiphany that she shared with me:

> I notice that every time I feel good and clear, and when I know exactly what it is I want and what I want to do, I end up experiencing an enormous amount of confusion when my boyfriend is telling me something totally different from what my heart knows. I have a lot of these experiences of feeling like I'm out of my power. And then, I end up feeling all these emotions that don't even seem like they belong to me. But the thing is, that confusion disappears when I'm on my own, and then I experience clarity and my truth.

Alana found herself constantly ricocheting between empowerment and disempowerment, between feeling good and feeling bad. As we sat down to disentangle the gnarly threads of her conditioning, it became clear that this pendulum swing between clarity and confusion was a huge red flag. In truth, she was being negatively impacted by the energy of the relationship, which dragged her down instead of lifting her up.

Unfortunately, the desire for deep love is not as straight-forward as we make it out to be. Just as Alana discovered, we need to understand the roots of our own trauma, which can lead us to dance with another person's trauma, so that we are simply reenacting old patterns and never getting to truly understand ourselves or the other in the context of a healthy love.

This tendency to dance with trauma is something that the psychologist Harville Hendrix talks about in great depth in his explanation of the "imago complex," which refers to an unconscious or idealized notion of love that we develop during childhood, and that, unbeknownst to us, remains unchanged when we become adults. According to imago relationship therapy, childhood experiences of abandonment, neglect, and conflict often recur in a marriage or committed relationship. It's possible to consciously work through all of these issues with another person and to fall in love with each other's core self, but first, we have to really look at and release the ways in which we may be hauling in our childhood baggage and thus blocking channels to our heart and to true love.

Before we can truly experience an ideal partner—the kind who contributes to our soul growth and doesn't just conform to ideas we unwittingly adopted about what love is supposed to look like—we must understand and release whatever pain and trauma around love we're holding in our hearts.

As many of my students and clients have discovered, it is possible to heal our trauma around love and to step into both a greater sense of self-love and a healthy connection with someone we would like to build a life with. Many of them, like Alana, come to me with the desire to get their ex back or build a stronger connection with the person they're already in a relationship with, although they might be going through a great deal of conflict and dysfunction. However, many of my clients and students usually end up breaking up with that person or letting go of toxic attachments once they do the deep inner work of determining who they truly are and what they want in love and life.

Usually, their desire to engage with a particular person is a desire that has emerged from a wounded, "younger" aspect. Some of them may think that their true heart's desire is love with somebody who is emotionally unavailable. But, as they often discover, this is more of a trauma response from the part of themselves that feels raw, abandoned, and inadequate, and that continues to seek validation in places where it can't be found. Unfortunately, this tendency to look for love in the places where we won't find it only serves to cement an unconscious belief that we are unworthy. We find ourselves gravitating toward unhealthy relationships, and our self-esteem and self-love decrease in the process. In fact, the sense of being unworthy might feel so familiar that it becomes "comfortable," and we even come to unconsciously prefer it to a more empowered state, which could feel scary and unfamiliar.

So, how do we stop attracting toxic relationships? There's no quick fix, but it all starts with understanding the unhealed wounds from childhood, which we continue to re-create in our future relationships. I highly recommend learning about your attachment style. Attachment theory comes from the psychologist John Bowlby, who suggeted that the bonds we have with our early caregivers pave the way for our style of connecting with romantic partners. According to Bowlby, there are four attachment styles:

Secure attachment: The style of attachment that comes when our physical and emotional needs are consistently and lovingly met by our caregivers. It's believed that when we experience this, it's

DO THIS BEFORE BED

more likely that we'll grow up to confidently seek and attract healthy relationships with emotionally secure, emotionally available partners.

Anxious attachment: If we grew up with caregivers whom we learned we couldn't rely on to care for our emotional and physical needs, we might develop an anxious attachment style. This could generate relationships in which we experience a lack of trust, or the need to cling to a partner because we fear abandonment or rejection.

Avoidant attachment: If we had neglectful or abusive caregivers, or if we were punished for even having emotional and physical needs, we may be the person in a relationship who tends to be emotionally guarded or attached. Often, people with an avoidant attachment style will attract people with an anxious attachment style, and vice versa—as attracting the opposite style tends to keep us set in our ways (e.g., "There they go again, being so clingy—I need space," or, "There they go again, emotionally abandoning me—I just can't trust them") rather than challenging our own patterns.

Disorganized attachment: People with this attachment style were typically raised with extremely erratic or unpredictable caregivers. This may have generated an enormous amount of fear and trauma. With this style, it becomes very difficult to develop healthy relationships. Although someone with a disorganized attachment style might want a close, intimate connection, they may tend to push away anyone who shows them care and love.

There's a lot of amazing work that psychologists and others have done around attachment theory, so if you're curious, I encourage you to look into the topic further, especially because there are so many correlations between our patterns of attraction and our childhood wounds.

For example, Alana determined that while her boyfriend was emotionally unavailable, this was part of a much older pattern that she had become accustomed to: That is, her father had been similarly unavailable throughout her childhood. She grew up barely seeing him because he worked 80 hours a week. When she was in fifth grade, he ended up leaving her mother for another woman and becoming even more absent in her life. Alana had learned that expressing her emotions and telling her dad she missed him made him angry; in fact, he'd often accuse her of guilt-tripping him and being ungrateful for all the sacrifices he'd made to ensure that she could live a comfortable, abundant life. Alana had come to normalize this experience to the extent that it was hard for her to take ownership over her true feelings, because doing so might mean experiencing abandonment at the hands of her loved ones. She continued to re-create this experience many times over in her future relationships.

When Alana and I talked about her past, she expressed regret and consternation that she had continued to attract unavailable men who mirrored her father's treatment of her when she was a child. I explained,

Try not to see this as a sign that something is 'wrong' with you. Actually, you have a great opportunity here! When we attract people who reveal to us the unhealed and unprocessed trauma we're still carrying, it gives us a chance to take a good, hard look at ourselves and address the wounds that are calling out for our healing attention.

In fact, this is true even when we're in a long-term relationship with someone we love. The people closest to us will generally be the ones who mirror back to us our wounds that are still in need of healing. One example of this lives in the story of my student Nicole, who came to me with a genuine desire to work things out with her husband of 20 years.

Nicole attended my workshops with the desire to fix her husband, Todd, whom she described as being an extreme sports fanatic and couch potato with whom emotional connection was very difficult. Nicole wanted to build a life in which spirituality and adventure were at the forefront. But Todd was not on board and felt that her pursuits were too "weird and woo-woo."

As I got to know Nicole better, I learned that she had a tendency to sacrifice her interests in order to keep the peace within all her relationships—something she'd grown up watching her people-pleaser mother do, in situation after situation. Nicole had come to a place in her life where she was tired of conforming to other people's ideas of who she should be. She expressed that she wanted to finally follow her heart instead of caving in to the pressure to just be "normal."

As Nicole and I worked to strengthen her connection to her spirituality and the energetic world, I helped her to stop worrying about whether or not Todd would come along for the ride or approve of her newfound interests. I find that if both partners are growth-oriented, a deeper and richer love is always possible. However, if people come in with the need to fix or change their partner, or with the belief that they need to sacrifice their own desires in order to keep the relationship, this is a surefire recipe for sabotage. It should never be about fixing another person but about working on your own healing. Once you do that, you'll discover very quickly whether or not your partner has the intention to grow with you.

Over time, Nicole's energy around Todd changed demonstrably. She was positively glowing in her spiritual pursuits. In addition, she was no longer focused on getting his approval. Todd's curiosity got the better of him, and he ended up coming to one of my workshops. He had seen a palpable transformation in Nicole's energy and confidence. Unbelievably, the couch potato sports fanatic ended up falling in love with energy healing. Today, Todd and Nicole are more in love than ever before. And even though he still loves watching games with his buddies, his emotional bandwidth has increased a thousandfold—plus, Nicole finally gets to have the spirited, emotionally mature relationship she has always wanted.

Another thing that I often suggest to clients who tell me they're in a relationship in which nothing is working is to try this experiment. For 30 days, they will focus on understanding their partner and expressing love in the ways their partner enjoys. This is especially important for the person who is the more conscious and attuned one within the relationship. They naturally have more bandwidth to express and give love.

I notice that people in relationships are often waiting for their partner to go first when it comes to expressing their love. It can build resentment over time when these expectations are not met. But the person who is capable of offering deep love has the power to permeate their relationship with positive, high-vibration energy. Once they've done this for 30 days, they can take note of whether their partner is reciprocating and doing their part to carry the relationship. If not, the person who put forth all that effort can reassess whether they want to continue.

Overall, the main thing I try to emphasize to the people I work with is that love requires a commitment to growth. It's not all fireworks and sunset walks and constant romance! At the same time, I think we have to be cautious and not buy into the belief that a good relationship is an uphill battle, because it's not. I've had some people insist that the ex they're trying to get back is their "soulmate" or "twin flame." If you're unfamiliar with either of these concepts, they refer to the notion that we have innate spiritual connections with certain people. I believe this is true, but I don't necessarily reduce it to a romantic concept. A soulmate can be a parent, a sibling, or a best friend. It could also be a romantic partner who isn't meant to stay in your life for the long haul, but who is a part of your deep life lessons. Unfortunately, lessons in love are often painful because they help us to uncover and acknowledge old wounds; at the same time, they're responsible for catapulting us to the next level of our spiritual growth. Ultimately, we are here to teach one another who we truly are and to live from our deepest potential.

I always suggest that when people are in a state of hurt and resentment over a relationship that didn't work out, they should ask themselves, "What lesson did I learn from this experience?" Sometimes, the lesson is as simple as, "I'm never going to do that again," but there is always at least one lesson to learn and to be grateful for.

The concept of "twin flames" has come into greater popularity, especially with the engine of social media. It can be described as an intense soul connection with someone who might be regarded as a person's other half. This can be a naive and spiritually immature way to look at relationships. The way I've encountered it, it has also created a justification for toxic connections that can result in unnecessary drama and turmoil.

Often, people who are proponents of the twin flame concept perpetuate the idea that friction and fighting in a relationship is normal or that spiritual growth means everything is supposed to be difficult. If this is the case, it is important to evaluate how our early concepts of love, including our attachment style, have contributed to the way we view our relationships. And if we continually experience conflicts in love, it's a good idea to ask ourselves if our heart is blocked. Remember, the heart has the largest energy field in the body, and when we allow ourselves to remove any blockages to the heart, it becomes a lot easier to attract all the amazing love that may have been difficult to find when we were vibrating at a lower frequency.

We are meant to experience an easy flow of love and to have healthy relationships that bolster our true worth and unlock our deepest potential. I have literally seen miracles occur in the lives of people who previously felt bereft of the deep love for which they yearned. The following practices will go a long way toward helping you heal any blockages that might be serving to keep you from the love you truly deserve.

THE PRACTICES

#1: Releasing Blockages from the Heart

If you're looking to attract love, say this affirmation at bedtime for at least two weeks straight. Place your hand over your heart and say, "I'm now ready to release all the pain from everyone who's ever hurt me in the past. I release it now. I release it all. I release it fully. I'm now ready for the love that's waiting for me—the love that will fill me up with energy and happiness. I am loved. I am worthy. I am enough."

As you do this, feel your heart fill up with a glowing pink or rose-colored light that helps to heal any wounded energy that may still be creating blockages within the largest energy field in your body, which is responsible for the flow of abundance and love.

#2: A Ritual for Healing the Wounds of Love

When I did this exercise, I attracted my wife, Mandy, within two weeks. Although timing may vary depending on the amount of healing you may need to do around your wounds of love, hundreds of my students have shared positive results with this ritual in just a short amount of time. You may choose to do the ritual once, but you can also do it several nights in a row in order to cement your intention to clear the wounds of love and attract the partner who's right for you.

First, write down the names of everyone who has ever hurt you in relationships. These can include romantic partners, as well as friends and family members. Allow yourself to feel your emotions, whatever they are.

Whether or not you feel that they deserve to be forgiven, you are now ready to release the energy of their actions and your perceptions toward them. Crumple up that piece of paper with all the names and burn it in a fire-safe bowl. Feel yourself releasing any residual pain or emotions that keep you connected to the toxic energy these relationships left in their wake. Say, "I release you, I release you, I release you."

Now, get another piece of paper and write down all the qualities you've ever wanted in a partner. What kind of character do they have? What are they drawn to? How do they deal with conflict? How do you help each other grow? What kind of life will you have with them? Be as detailed as you like. Then say, "I surrender to the highest good of all involved.

This or something better is coming my way." Fold that piece of paper up and put it away.

Finally, commit to doing at least three things you love this week—activities that you're fond of and that make your heart sing. In a way, you are committing to dating and romancing yourself, to falling in love with the unique and beautiful soul that you are. A deep commitment to self-love enables us to attract a healthier, higher-vibration relationship—and faster than we otherwise would. Therefore, the person who is exactly right for you will find you . . . and not from a state of woundedness, but from a state of mutual empowerment and clarity.

MORE RESOURCES AND FREE DOWNLOADS

Strengthen your relationships with love and con-nection! Listen to the **Heart Opening Meditation Audio** to cultivate deeper love and compassion for yourself and others. Listen here:

https://dothisbeforebed.com/resource

CHAPTER 16

MENTAL FOCUS AND CLARITY

One of the guiding factors in my own life as I've moved from creating one business after another, and helping other people turn their ideas into reality, is the development of a laser-sharp focus. Mental focus and the clarity to manifest our ideas in the physical plane is a huge aspect of a success mindset. Everyone from Napoleon Hill to my good friend Tony Robbins have said something along the lines of, "Where attention goes, energy flows," and for many successful people, developing intentional ways to channel our attention and energy is the key to the kingdom of well-being.

This is where I want to emphasize that nothing about the success mindset of mental focus is about magical thinking or believing that things are simply going to fall into place if we imagine everything working out. Yes, visualization can certainly help, and we can also make the path a lot easier for ourselves when we have a high vibration that brings our manifestations into reality with greater speed. At the same time, we need to do our part to ensure that we're harnessing and using our energy more effectively and efficiently—that we're making it work for us rather than against us.

The ability to make decisions that hone our focus toward our goals and dreams is something a lot of people struggle with. Of course, we have tons of distractions to thank for that; moreover, most of us are not taught the ABCs of manifestation, which include generating a greater sense of focus in our lives and being very intentional about how we are spending our time. We're encouraged to be multitaskers who can do and think a lot of things all at once, as if we're presiding over our own three-ring circus. Unfortunately, research demonstrates that multitasking isn't actually as efficient as the old-school performance gurus made it out to be. Dividing our energy among a lot of different tasks can make it harder to process information, and it can also be debilitating for our memory and problem-solving skills in the long term.

All this is compounded by the fact that we're left drifting in a sea of options and other challenges that can make it hard to stay on task with anything that may be very important to us. Did you know that more than 95 percent of New Year's resolutions are broken before January 15?

Let me clue you in to one of my number-one suggestions for maintaining a New Year's resolution: Do what you can to get into (and stay in!) a high vibration.

So often, when people are focused on their resolutions, they're spiraling in shame, guilt, and fear. But what if you were to approach your resolution with a sense of excitement and joyful anticipation of the person you'll be on the other side? This is extremely important, because when you're feeling positive and riding on a high vibration, you won't have any difficulty following through on your resolution. The decisions you make will be aligned with that high vibration that wants only the best for you.

Of course, accountability is also important here. Let's say one of the decisions you make is that you're going to hire a personal trainer to get in shape. Perhaps you can tell three or four supportive people in your life about your goals, so that they can hold you accountable, especially when you lack motivation. When you have a combination of accountability and a high-vibration state that leads you into the attitude of "I get to do this" (rather than "I have to do this," or "I should do this," which always feels like a drag), what will end up happening is that you'll no longer be dependent on motivation alone to get you to the finish line. You'll set the right conditions so that what you want inevitably becomes what you get.

Again, I realize this is all easier said than done. But what I've found is that the real problem tends to occur when our energies are fractured off in multiple directions rather than focused and gathered, then launched in the direction of what we want. This is why I tell my students and clients that it's important to create energetic containers for ourselves. The way it works is, if you're in a high vibration and all your energy is directed into one potent energetic container, you'll get the thing you want really quickly.

Let me give you a simple example. I ask you, "What's your dream vacation?" Very likely, the perfect destination immediately pops into your head. But then, I say, "I want you to go there in the next 30 to 90 days." What does your mental chatter tell you? You might reply, "Well, I really want to go to Bora Bora, but it's not possible. I can only do it when I get time off. I have so many other commitments and other things I need to do."

In other words, you're telling me that you have about 5 percent of your energy focused on making your dream vacation a reality, because other things have taken precedence. In fact, 95 percent of your energy is planted in dozens of other containers. There's nothing wrong with that (you get to decide what you want, after all!), but it's important to remember that *major key*

energy is most potent when it is focused and directed, and it fills a container all the way rather than halfway.

I work with a lot of ADHD clients who tell me that they often become distracted, and it is difficult to channel all their energy into a single container. I usually hear this when I ask them the question: "What is the one thing you absolutely know will move your life forward right now?" Perhaps it's a goal they have set in business, health, spirituality, relationships, or another area of their life. This can inspire people to gain a greater sense of clarity that naturally helps them to narrow their focus and build a strong energetic container for it. The simple reminder of what matters to us helps us to take the necessary steps to designing a life that prioritizes those things. But if someone is doing a variety of different things, and they're constantly getting distracted, it's not very likely that they'll move the needle on any of those endeavors.

Self Mastery !!!

So, coming back to essentials often requires asking ourselves: "What's the one thing that is essential to my sense of well-being and accomplishment? And how can I prioritize it?" Responding to these two questions and enacting measures in our lives that help us to generate the answers is one of my personal definitions for self-mastery. When we turn on the energy of our mental focus, it will have the right amount of momentum to carry us along.

I often work with students and clients who tell me that they have difficulty setting and sticking to goals, even when they attempt to build strong energetic containers, or to develop a high-vibration state with lots of accountability factored in. When this happens, internal conflict is usually the major culprit holding us back. We say we want something, but our "why" isn't big enough. In order to resolve an internal conflict, which often comes from the beliefs we establish early in life, our inspiration, or our why, needs to *my why ? Needs to Be BIG ENOUGH*

be big enough to carry us along. (You can go back to the practice from Chapter 8, "What's My Why?" if you feel you're experiencing this right now.)

Inspiration is a high-vibration state, like love and gratitude, whereas the internal conflicts that keep us from placing all our mental focus on what we want often come from fear and self-doubt. We must have a driving force that is stronger than anything that keeps us stuck. Of course, fear is not usually logical. It's an emotional response from an unhealed part of us, which is why we must do our part to heal the emotional charges of the past so that we are actually aligned with what we want for ourselves.

So far, we've covered the fact that our lives are impacted by the decisions we make about where we will be spending our energy; essentially, our decisions impact our reality. If you look at your decisions over the last month, year, or several years, you'll gain a deeper understanding of the values and beliefs that have driven those decisions. But a lot of times, we're on autopilot. We do things that we don't fully understand, and we don't necessarily recognize the patterns of behavior that get us particular results.

In order to have freedom, we need to move beyond operating on autopilot. We need to understand *exactly* what drives our decisions. What are we inspired by? In addition, are our decisions driven by fear or are they driven by love? Decisions driven by love tend to be more potent and to deliver greater joy, happiness, and a sense of purpose, whereas decisions driven by fear tend to perpetuate a lot of the patterns from our childhood, including our wounds.

Aside from understanding what drives your decisions, it's a good idea to be aware of the consequences of the decisions you're making, and how focusing your energy has ripple effects on the world around you. I work with a lot of people who are intense, fast-paced executives who are extremely fixated on their goals. This isn't necessarily a bad thing, but it causes problems when it gets in the way of something that's important to them, such as their family life.

Now, what I would like to suggest here might be a little controversial, but I am really not a fan of the so-called work/life balance. Sometimes, in order to get to where we want to go, we must allow ourselves to be taken along by the momentum of our inspiration. I'm a big believer in following momentum in our life if it's present. For example, I often get into periods where I'm working 100 hours a week, but this is a source of fulfillment and joy for me because I'm doing work that allows me to be in service to others and that I feel nourished by. I find myself in a state of effortless flow. However, if the momentum is not there, I recognize it's a good time to rest.

We have to figure out where we are in our lives. Often, inspiration, when it's present, allows us to burn the proverbial candle at both ends without feeling depleted or exhausted. We have to also consider our general nature. For example, I've met people who can meditate for three to four hours a day, which is an important aspect of their lives, but they're usually not busy simultaneously building a business in which they're responsible for multiple projects or they're managing lots of people. Then, on the other side of that are people like Tony Robbins, who gets about three hours of sleep and meditates for a few minutes a day, while the rest of his time is spent constantly on the go. Tony may not be typical, but this is a speed that honestly works for him. You need to find the speed that works for you and go with it.

So, we know that mental focus involves the ability to make the right decisions and to understand why we're making those decisions. But what happens when you find it difficult to make a decision and your mind is ping-ponging all over the place? This isn't unusual, and as I've alluded to, an important aspect of mental focus is finding clarity for ourselves. A lot of times, I meet people who have difficulty making a decision and they go through a state of analysis paralysis, where they get caught up in all the pros and cons until they're cross-eyed and have no clue what to do. Typically, there's a reason they don't want to take action. And—you guessed it—a lot of times, that reason is associated with fear.

Jaya is a client I'm working with who's deeply unhappy in her job, but she doesn't want to leave because she's afraid of what might be on the other side. "What if I end up being out of work? What if there's nothing better out there for me?" she has asked. She's usually completely okay with taking decisive actions that move her toward her goals, but this single fear is stopping her and keeping her in a miserable state of limbo.

Again, this is a matter of understanding *why* we do the things we do. What is the deeper motivation, and what is the belief behind it? As we dug deeper, we recognized that Jaya's indecision came from both of her parents being entrepreneurs who made a lot of spontaneous decisions about their business that ended up having negative repercussions for the entire family. As a result, Jaya grew up feeling paralyzed by the fear of trusting her gut; she had seen her parents do exactly that, and it had turned out badly for everyone involved! However, as Jaya came to realize, what her parents called "following our gut" didn't really have much to do with developing a solid relationship with their inner voices; it had a lot more to do with their immaturity, impulsiveness, and lack of business savvy, as their risks weren't well calculated at all.

So, just as we need to know *why* we make the decisions we make, we also need to dig deep and discover what exactly is stalling us and keeping us mentally fogged and paralyzed.

I couldn't help Jaya until she understood what was blocking her. And in general, nobody can be motivated to do anything if they don't understand their blockages.

Also, getting to clarity goes back to setting boundaries. I often tell people that our environment is very important. Many times, the reason we're not clear is that our environment is filled with noise and contradictions. We might have a lot of external stimuli bombarding us, or we might be tangled up in a web of other people's beliefs. It can be hard to differentiate between that noise and the voice of our soul.

I suggested to Jaya that she simply take a day to go to a completely different environment where it was calm, and all the external noise of her job could fall away. This was very important, especially since Jaya hadn't taken a "vacation" in several years. She was resistant at first but accepted the challenge. This simple experience helped Jaya to face her fears with greater awareness and to realize that she had developed a story—about the importance of remaining in a "stable" job, even if it was challenging—that was contributing to her unhappiness.

She sat with her soul, and by the time she came back, she knew what her decision was: It was time to leave her dysfunctional job. At this point, I didn't encourage her to jump out of the frying pan and into the fire. I knew that her nervous system required some kind of contingency plan for such a big move, so we came up with a timeline, as well as ways for her to direct her energy so that she'd be fine on the other side of the decision. Today, Jaya is in a completely different work environment that allows her greater access to her intuition and clarity. She not only realized what she needed to do, but she also had the confidence and clarity to move forward and make the best decision for herself.

THE PRACTICES

#1: Create Your Not-to-Do List

Most people have a to-do list. However, one of the most important things I've ever done in my life is to keep a not-to-do list. For at least three nights, write out the things you intend to stop doing because they rob you of your energy and power, and they compromise your efforts to build a strong energetic container. This doesn't have to be a long list; in fact, a short yet potent list is perfect! Read your list out loud, then close your eyes. For two to three minutes, sense, feel, and imagine yourself giving up the behaviors that don't serve you. Feel your time, energy, attention, and other resources being freed up for better things. Release your intention to the universe, and watch your energy begin to flow into a potent container that'll move your life forward in beautiful ways!

#2: What's the One Thing?

If you're dealing with overstimulation or too many options, for three nights in a row, ask yourself the question, "What's the one thing I need to be focused on in order to move my life forward in the best possible way?" Journal about it for at least 15 minutes, using freewriting to get your thoughts down, which will lead to greater clarity. Instead of reading your responses right away, read them after three nights. Your writing will generate insights about what you need to concentrate on. On the fourth night, write down the one area where you've decided to place your focus. Give yourself a timeline. It doesn't need to be very long. It could be that you'll focus all your efforts for a week, or a month. Choose what feels best to you, but also what feels attainable.

I always say, "Be a laser, not a lamp," when it comes to mental focus that we reserve for things that are vitally important to us. Close your eyes, and for a few minutes, concentrate on visualizing yourself doing what you know needs to be done in order to meet your intention. Allow yourself to drift off to sleep, inspired by your vision.

#3: Accountability Journal

After you've worked on the second practice, maintain an accountability journal that you spend at least five minutes writing in at the end of the day. You can use the same journal you've been keeping to chart your progress through all the practices—just make a special section in the journal that focuses specifically on the "one thing" you've identified, for the duration you've agreed to. You may wish to fill this section of the journal with things like advice from accountability partners whom you've enlisted to share progress with, summaries of videos and books you've consumed that are related to the thing you're focusing on, and any notes about your progress.

In general, keeping a journal like this encourages you to make progress toward your focus. I have also found that such a journal enables me to "get it done" much faster than I would otherwise, because where I've chosen to direct my energy is at the top of my mind. So, something it might take a year to do can be condensed considerably if you're actively charting your progress.

Please note that your focus doesn't have to be on creating something tangible. I've had clients and students dedicate their accountability journal to healing an emotional wound. Jaya kept a journal around healing the wound of losing a sense of security at a young age, which helped her to work through her fears and attract a new job from a place of love.

MORE RESOURCES AND FREE DOWNLOADS

Boost your mental focus and clarity! Listen to the **Focus and Concentration Meditation Audio** to sharpen your mind and clear mental fog. Listen here:

https://dothisbeforebed.com/resource

CHAPTER 17

PEACE AND HAPPINESS

One of the primary impetuses for people coming to my energy school or seeking to work with me one-on-one is a very simple statement I've heard more times than I can count: "I just want to be happy."

For so many people today, there's a sense of joy that's missing. The old spark they used to feel in their lives is gone; in some cases, it was never there to begin with. Many times, they come to me because they're tired of the drama. They're tired of the setbacks. All they want to experience is a sense of peace, of simplicity, of getting back to basics and embracing a joy that is much more enduring than the circumstances of their lives. It should seem easy enough to access, but we have billion-dollar industries centered on exploiting people's insecurities and telling them that they'll be happy if they only attain X, Y, or Z. Moreover, we tend to have a lot of ideas and memories attached to what peace and happiness are supposed to look like. This means we might miss out altogether on the fact that these are high-vibration states of being that are generated from deep within us.

Although it can be a useful exercise to define the various aspects of how we want our life to look, our definitions can hold us back if we are limiting what we think peace and happiness are meant to be and how they should manifest. A lot of times, we believe that we need to do something in order to be peaceful and happy. But we can redefine this state as something that is possible to attain *today*, in the here and now. This is a way of outsmarting the discursive mind while also feeding the solution-seeking mind, which is inspired to move toward answers. When we think of ways in which we can experience peace and happiness *right now*, we feel empowered rather than debilitated.

One of my clients, Amelia, came to me because she was moving through a long depression. Medication and therapy had only nominally worked for her. When I asked her what she wanted in life, she said, "I just want to be happy."

"What's stopping you?" I inquired.

"Well, I'm on the board of all these amazing organizations that do such great things for my community," she said. "But it never feels like my contribution is enough. Between raising three kids and managing my and my husband's four rental properties, I feel like I can't fully devote myself to my board work, which is my passion and purpose."

"What about that work makes you happy?"

"I only truly feel happy when I know I'm being of service to others, when I'm giving back to my community. I end up thinking about ways I could do this and staying up late at night, imagining the projects I could suggest to the other board members. But I'm not doing as much as I could be. I think if I felt I could be doing more of it, I'd actually be happy. It just doesn't seem like I'll ever have the time or energy to pursue that work to the fullest extent."

I could tell that Amelia was burned out, so it surprised me that her desire to be happy was followed up by the strange rationale that she could *only* be happy if she was giving all her free time to her charitable work. This came from a noble aspiration—the desire to give back to her community—but

I could sense that Amelia had too many rules around the required conditions for her happiness.

The funny thing is, although our conditions might contribute to greater happiness (for example, I know plenty of people who need a daily dose of art, exercise, nature, etc., to feel a deeper sense of well-being and fulfillment), this isn't always the case. The conditions and rules we tend to set are ones we inherited with respect to what will make us happy.

In Amelia's case, being happy was attached to her perceptions of being a good person. Amelia had told herself early in life that she could only be happy and peaceful when she was helping others, but her idea of helping others was volunteering every day, even when she was tired. She believed that she needed to sacrifice her own health, which is definitely not what peace and happiness are about! She was way too fixated on making more room for her charitable work that she couldn't see it was actually making her miserable and keeping her from finding joy in the simple things.

Amelia had to deeply investigate all the unrealistic rules she'd created, and why. Many of them were geared toward making the search for peace and happiness longer, harder, and more unattainable . . . perhaps because some part of her actually *feared* being peaceful and happy.

We underwent a shift when Amelia began to ask herself, "What can I do today and in this moment in order to feel peaceful and happy?"

As I told her, instant gratification goes a long way. "Don't delay your happiness—experience it today," I suggested.

Peace and happiness are soul-level needs. They're literally like oxygen for the spirit, so it's important not to deprive ourselves of them, because they are so essential.

Amelia began to acknowledge that her board positions were leading to more stress than joy, so she gradually shifted her focus away from all her self-sacrificing charitable work. She went back to an old passion, painting, and started to create beautiful artwork every day. She also began to appreciate spending more time with friends and family, and to take time to wake up and smell the roses (literally!) outside her window.

I noticed over the next few months that Amelia, who had constantly walked around with a pinched and concerned expression on her face as she was ever in search of things to clean up and fix, began to loosen up and not take herself so seriously.

"I realized that I never truly felt satisfied," Amelia said about her transformation to a more easeful way of being. "Even when I told myself I was happy because I was being productive and helping others, I always felt restless."

Amelia went on to tell me, "I realized that some of this had to do with the desire to exert control over my life, even my peace and happiness and what they were supposed to look like."

As we contemplated her patterns, they made sense. Amelia had gone through a turbulent childhood during which she constantly moved around, from foster home to foster home. She always had the sense that the rug would be pulled out from beneath her at any moment. Over time, she had become accustomed to the struggle, and to being in survival mode. While her childhood gave her an extraordinary amount of empathy and resilience, it was hard for her to relax. Although she lived an abundant life, nothing she'd created ever felt like enough. She had a strong sense of responsibility when it came to helping others, but rather than bringing her genuine happiness, it had created a greater sense of not-enoughness, as she constantly doubted her contributions.

Amelia had fallen prey to the idea that putting a lot of pressure on herself was fuel for a fulfilling life. But this pressure was always accompanied by negative self-talk. At a time in her life when she was in survival mode, the voice of her inner critic was what helped her to "be the best I could possibly be." It worked for a while, but it wasn't sustainable. Amelia was stuck in an old paradigm that she had long ago outgrown. She had simply internalized it as a part of herself, believing there was no other way to operate. She had defended that pattern—and a set of false rules around what she needed in order to be happy—instead of healing it.

Together, we spent several months of deep healing work centered around prioritizing her joy. I constantly get messages from people on Instagram and Facebook, and funny enough, most of them are not even from my clients and students. I was overjoyed to receive a message from Amelia's daughter, Alina, recently. She wrote, "I don't know what you did, but my mother is finally relaxed, carefree, and happy. She used to always be on the go, worried about something or someone that needed to be taken care of. Now, I feel like I finally get to have the happy-go-lucky, relaxed mother I've always wanted. How did you do it?"

What I try to explain to people is that peace and happiness are often the by-products of our deep healing work. When we get out of our own way, they naturally arise, because they are the primordial conditions of our spirit. Again, all of this comes back to the message of healing that is one of the core themes of this book. When we learn to transmute and neutralize the stories of the past, the ones that keep us stuck in false beliefs and arbitrary rules, we naturally step into our birthright: everlasting peace and happiness that cannot be compromised, negated, or taken away.

THE PRACTICES

#1: Get to the Core Feeling

Instead of defining your conditions for peace and happiness, focus on the emotional state, the core feeling, associated with them. If you have difficulty finding it, summon a memory of being happy and at peace, even if it was very simple, like going for a walk on a beautiful morning. For at least three nights in a row, evoke this memory and visualize it in detail. What did you experience? Engage all your senses so that you can literally anchor the feelings associated with that experience in your body. After a few minutes, let the details of the experience go, and simply let the core feeling of peace and happiness circulate throughout your heart and your overall energy. Speak the affirmation, "I attract and radiate this peace and happiness, easily and effortlessly." Connecting with the high-vibration state of peace and happiness will naturally start to magnetize more experiences, situations, people, and places that mirror it right back to you.

#2: Your Joy Journal

Just as people are encouraged to keep a gratitude journal, it can be powerful to keep a joy journal. This is a running list you can keep in your journal of everything that brought you joy during the day, as well as anything that generally enables you to feel a sense of joy. By writing down what makes you feel joy, you'll take yourself into a high vibration that will have ripple effects in your life.

Your joy journal can comprise lots of things, big and small (e.g., playing with your puppy, watching the spring flowers pop up, watching a silly movie, having an impromptu dance party with your kids, etc.). The idea is to recognize that it's possible to experience joy in many ways, rather than constraining ourselves to a set of arbitrary rules and conditions. And when we take the time to recognize the little pockets of joy during our day, we start to realize that joy is truly the water in which we swim and the air that we breathe.

At bedtime, I like to spend at least three minutes jotting down the things that gave me joy that day. Often, while I'm doing this, I imagine that the energy of joy is flowing down from the cosmos and filling up my body with a vibrant pink light. As I do this, I feel myself making more and more room for joyful experiences, and committing to the energy of enduring peace and happiness.

MORE RESOURCES AND FREE DOWNLOADS

Cultivate inner peace and lasting joy! Listen to the **Inner Peace Meditation Audio** to find calm and happiness within. Listen here:

https://dothisbeforebed.com/resource

CHAPTER 18

PURPOSE AND CONTRIBUTION

I have no doubt that if you're reading this book, you've probably asked yourself the million-dollar question, "What's my purpose?," more times than you can count! In general, the students and clients who come to me have huge hearts. Aside from healing their own limiting beliefs, they genuinely want to inspire others and aid in the transformation and healing of other people. Many of them feel a sense of urgency around accessing their greater purpose.

Ironically, that sense of urgency can sometimes hold us back even more, as it can take our attention away from the gift of the present moment and the possibility that contribution isn't so much about quantity, but rather, the quality of our presence.

Moreover, purpose is something that is constantly evolving. It's not just one thing or activity; indeed, our sense of purpose changes over time. Overall, purpose is context-dependent, and you can probably identify a lot of different purposes you have experienced throughout your life, even though there might be a few golden threads that tie them all together.

Often, your sense of purpose will be connected to what you're working on healing in your own life. As you heal, you have a lot more capacity to give. For example, I have a student whose purpose is to help rehabilitate traumatized children who have experienced an unstable home life. He had a similar experience growing up, and he feels a lot of satisfaction in helping kids to harness deep self-love. This is part of the many layers of his own healing. Just like our experience of life, purpose comes with many different layers and stages.

My wife, Mandy, was focused on helping men to heal for many years because it also enabled her to heal her own father wounds. But when she felt she had healed her father wounds, her purpose shifted to working with women, which then enabled Mandy to heal her mother wounds. Currently, she's more focused on philanthropy and children.

It's also possible to remain in one area of purpose work for a long time, simply because you're passionate about it, but typically, once you heal something within yourself that drew you to that work in the first place, you expand to the next level or layer.

Of course, a lot of times, people don't necessarily know their purpose. I have many students who walk through the doors of my energy healing school with the intention to connect more deeply with their sense of purpose, but what I often find is that it's not actually purpose they're looking for. What they're looking for is clarity. They want to be able to answer the question, "Who am I?" They know they're meant to do something bigger, but they don't know how that's supposed to unfold.

A lot of that confusion has to do with being disconnected from a greater awareness of their soul. Often, people believe that if they feel lost, the solution is to find a sense of purpose, but that isn't a long-term fix. In truth, they are seeking the deeper essence of who they are as a soul. They've lost connection with their authentic self, typically because they've had to wear so many masks over the course of their life, in order to survive and fit in. But once people feel that deeper sense of connection to their soul essence, purpose naturally comes.

This is why I often encourage my students to keep asking, "Who am I?" Because when you're aligned with who you truly are, your purpose becomes clear. In fact, everything you do becomes purposeful and purpose-driven, because you're bringing all of yourself into your life.

Ultimately, to use a cliché, we're human beings and not human doings. Purpose is really more of a state of being than something we do. Again, it's fine to engage in activities that bring us a sense of purpose, but this isn't ultimately sustainable because our activities are likely to change due to the conditions of our lives. We won't be destabilized by these changes as long as we are connected to the aspect of ourselves that is enduring. The most purpose-driven people I've ever met know themselves extremely well, to the extent that everything they do affects everyone around them because it's so potent.

Everyone might define purpose in their own individual way, but for me, purpose is a state of alignment with your core essence. Again, there's nothing wrong with channeling your purpose in specific ways, but when we get overly fixated on the specifics, they can hinder us more than help us. As I mentioned in Chapter 17, I encounter a lot of people like my client Amelia, who just wanted to be of service. She has an enormous heart, but she also had a lot of rules. She was doing important work, but deep down, it was stressing her out because nothing she did ever felt like enough.

A lot of times, when people think about purpose, they believe that it has to be associated with a job or something they're doing with the majority of their time. They don't believe they're purposeful unless they're meeting their rules about what purpose is supposed to look like—meaning the things they do throughout the day don't end up counting in their book. This can cause people to be overly self-critical, and it also leads them to inaccurately conclude that they're not being purposeful. It makes them feel more lost, and it takes them away from their true self.

I want to be very clear that I am not suggesting people refrain from dreaming big and setting powerful, even challenging, goals for themselves. However, I think this begs the question: How are you defining "dreaming big" in the first place?

I work with a lot of people who view life through a lens of constant growth and potential, especially in terms of the magnitude of their impact. I would define myself as one of those people! This isn't a bad quality, but it's only one way of being in your life and processing the world. I've also met a lot of other people who are much more concerned with simple yet potent acts of kindness that may only touch a small handful of people, yet they know this is enough because it has ripple effects.

Again, this goes back to understanding your nature, rather than being driven by external ideas about success. How do you get clear about your nature? I suggest reconnecting with the things you absolutely love to do. Many times, this is associated with your inner child and the things that brought you joy when you were younger. But more than this, understanding your nature is about getting to the root emotion of what it feels like when you are in a state of effortless authenticity. When you identify with that state, you are being purposeful because you are connecting with your essence.

Another way I'd like to frame this is that purpose is twofold, in that it includes both our soul and our human dimensions. Our soul purpose is to connect with our authenticity.

Our human purpose is to engage in the activities that help us make authentic connection with ourselves more frequent, until it becomes our primary experience in life. Often, our human purpose is associated with helping others and with clearing trauma, so that our soul can flow through us with greater ease.

I have a student named Lareena who discovered that her sense of purpose was something she could connect with by engaging with her soul lessons and what she most needed to learn. (You can go back to the third practice in Chapter 5 if you want a refresher on learning your soul lessons.) Lareena often had the experience of feeling unfulfilled as soon as her head hit the pillow at night and as soon as she woke up in the morning, because she felt she wasn't giving the gift she was here to give. She wasn't sharing her purpose.

She admitted to me, "At the same time, it's so hard for me to even focus on sharing my purpose when I have so many days of just feeling worried about paying the bills. I also work at a job where people are toxic and are draining my energy. So, how can I focus on giving to others when my needs aren't even met?"

Lareena and I talked in great detail about some of the limiting beliefs that had created such a sense of toxicity and overwhelm in her life. She shared with me, "I always felt like an outcast, ever since I was young. I was a black sheep in my family . . . always something of a weirdo. I didn't belong anywhere."

That sense of not belonging had haunted Lareena throughout her life, such that she tended to reproduce conditions in which she was constantly the fish out of water, always dealing with the stress of being around people who didn't understand her. With all her energy focused on this, it certainly felt difficult to fulfill a sense of purpose.

I told Lareena, "What if you're here to learn lessons and to experience things that may not feel fun but will eventually help you to give to others in the way you want to?"

I explained that, when it comes to soul lessons, there's always going to be a significant one we're called to learn right now—and nothing in our life will work out until we focus on learning the lesson. For example, our finances or relationships might feel like they're in a state of falling apart, which usually means we need to redirect our attention!

I suggested that Lareena work with the nightly practice of asking for her soul lessons. This was when she realized that one of her big lessons was accepting her "inner weirdo" and recognizing that even if she felt out of place, she still inherently belonged. In fact, her unique perspective was powerful when it came to offering welcoming guidance to other people who similarly felt like they didn't belong. It was time for Lareena to release the heavy burden associated with her belief that she didn't belong, so she worked with intensive self-love practices, as well as healing the wounds of being the black sheep in her family—being the tattooed, pierced, outspoken, quirky, sarcastic, sensitive person in a sea of conservative people.

Lareena quickly discovered that she had a natural gift for counseling people who were going through difficult transitions and learning to stand in their truth, especially when they faced pressure to conform to the status quo. But in order to be there for others, Lareena was being called to heal. It was very uncomfortable, but she bravely leaned in to her soul lessons. Within a few months, her life felt completely different. In fact, her toxic workplace changed dramatically, and new people who were more aligned with Lareena's soul-driven way of being were hired.

"When I look back, I feel that everything changed," Lareena told me. "When I began to focus on my soul lesson and when I started to take action on healing, everything became brighter. It isn't even that my life changed all that dramatically. I'm still at the same job, still living in the same place, still encountering the same struggles as before. But my relationships are really different. I have new friends at work who are supportive. I'm finding people who have similar passions. I'm doing things that are uplifting to my soul. It's almost like I haven't changed what I'm feeding my body, but I've changed what I'm feeding my mind and spirit and heart. The positivity is louder than before, and I'm more grounded and alive than I've been in years. I wouldn't have called this 'purpose' before, but I truly feel that's the vibration I'm living in."

What Lareena discovered is that each of us is a manifestation of infinite light. We're born with a purpose—a message or a gift to share. When we are living from our wounds, which is true for a great majority of us, we forget who we are. We forget that we are light.

Thankfully, we can use the practices in this book to guide us into a state of healing, so that the blockages that keep our soul essence from coming through are removed and we can feel the infinite light sending greater beauty and purposefulness into our life.

THE PRACTICES

#1: Let Your Story Be Your Guide

It doesn't matter what you've experienced in your past—whether it's been traumatic or painful or frustrating—because your next job or your second chapter is coming. All of us are called to greatness, and if we encounter suffering, that's only because we are being prepared to focus on our purpose work and mission. For three nights in a row, reframe the pain of the past and consider that it's here to show you what you need to resolve, so that you can heal and also help others heal. When you reframe your past pain, you give it a purpose. It no longer debilitates you or makes you sad; it becomes the fuel in your engine that inspires you and helps you to inspire others. For a few minutes, journal about it, using the following guiding questions:

What is the story I'm telling myself about my past?

What are the most painful parts of my story?

How can I reframe that pain so that it becomes my purpose?

For example, maybe you struggled with addiction in the past—that was the old chapter. Maybe you reframe that story so that it's about resilience and learning to compassionately face your shadows so that you can help others to do the same. After you've journaled for 10–15 minutes or so, close your eyes and imagine that this "new chapter" of your life that holds your purpose is enclosed in a bubble of white light. Let that bubble of white light drift up, up, and into the energetic realm, where it can be blessed by the divine and more easily birthed into your life.

#2: Who Am I?

Right before you go to sleep, journal on or spend a few minutes thinking about the following questions:

- Who am I today? *(Think about your values and how they align with your external world—the things you do, the people with whom you interact, your general lifestyle, etc. How might the closest people in your life describe you? Be honest about your strengths, as well as any areas that might need more attention. There's no such thing as "weaknesses," as we are always a work in progress, and change begins with awareness.)*

- Who was I yesterday? *(You can choose a specific time period of your life, such as your teenage years, your early twenties, or even last year. How does this compare with who you are today? What are you proud of from your past? What are the lessons that you may have learned through difficult experiences?)*

- Who do I want to be? *(What are your dreams? Try not to focus too much on your "bucket list" of desired accomplishments; instead, think more about the quality of experiences you'd like to have and what you want to bring to the world around you. Maybe you want to be more courageous, or more generous, or a loving role model to the young people in your life.)*

The simple act of asking these questions (and answering them with compassion and positivity, not judgment) primes the pump and makes you much more receptive to living your life with intentionality and purpose.

MORE RESOURCES AND FREE DOWNLOADS

Align with your life purpose! Listen to the **Life Purpose Meditation Audio** to gain clarity on your soul's mission and contribution. Listen here:

https://dothisbeforebed.com/resource

CHAPTER 19

SELF-LOVE AND SELF-CARE

Self-love and self-care are two of the hardest concepts for even the most spiritual people to comprehend. This is because most of us have grown up in environments where we are encouraged to be externally oriented. It can be difficult to turn our gaze back upon ourselves and to recognize that we are just as deserving of our own love and care as the other people in our lives.

Let's define what these concepts mean. Self-love is a deep internal belief that we are worthy of our own compassion and acceptance. Self-care is self-love in action, which we demonstrate by attending to all aspects of our well-being. Again, none of this has anything to do with being selfish or egocentric. In fact, it is about recognizing our own intrinsic wholeness, so that we can bring this to all our experiences and relationships.

I've often found that the people who have the most difficulty with self-love and self-care are parents, especially moms, many of whom comprise my audience of students and clients.

Moms can often get overly caught up doing too many things for too many other people, and they forget that they also need to prioritize themselves, to choose their own joy, well-being, and wholeness. When they do this, they're actually modeling what it's like to put themselves first, so that they are giving from a filled rather than an empty cup.

If you're a parent, you are a role model to your children. Over time, as they watch your behaviors toward yourself, which includes your capacity to prioritize your needs and desires consistently and repeatedly, they will eventually learn how to do what it is you're doing. So, when you wake up in the morning and go through your day, remember that there are little eyes watching you everywhere you go. I know that this has been especially important to my wife, Mandy, who experienced a lot of trauma in her homelife at a young age. By the time she was 12 years old, Mandy was self-aware enough to actually write herself a letter listing out all the things she wouldn't do to her kids when she became a parent. This is a great exercise, but I routinely find that people who swear they'll be different from their parents often forget that being the "perfect" parent (no such thing, by the way) doesn't mean putting yourself last. So often, we're conditioned to believe that parenting means allowing ourselves and our own needs and desires to be placed on the back burner. However, when we reflect on the fact that our kids often unconsciously absorb the behaviors we're displaying toward ourselves, it changes everything.

I was very unhappy in my first marriage, but it took me years to leave. My ex-wife and I fought all the time, and I felt emotionally worn down. On some level, I was a shell of a human being and simply didn't believe that I deserved any better. But when my son was born and I saw the subtle and overt ways in which he mimicked his mom's behavior, I thought about how I would feel if he emulated me by staying in a relationship that caused him pain. That was when a light went on inside of me. Even though I had felt like half a person (and had gotten accustomed to it) for many years,

I finally had the impetus to change. Our children do what we do, not what we say—and now I had a good reason to do better and have higher standards.

Because so many of my clients and students are extremely empathetic, highly sensitive people, I've discovered that a great way to steer them toward greater self-love and self-care is to have them ask a simple question: "Am I treating myself the same way I would treat my child or my best friend?" If the answer is no, this means we need to do something different.

I want to emphasize that there is no one formula or recipe for self-love and self-care. For example, I have worked with people who realized that "tough love" and exercising the utmost discipline in moving toward their goals was the ultimate form of caring for themselves; and I've worked with others who recognized that giving themselves a break and doing less made them feel better about themselves than they had in a long time.

However, one of the common denominators I've discovered across different types of people is that self-love and self-care begin with a thorough evaluation of the way we talk to ourselves. Often, we are unkind to ourselves without even realizing it. When I see someone engaged in self-defeating dialogue (e.g., "I'm so stupid," "I shouldn't have done that," "I should have known better"), I ask them to pause and consider what they are saying. Operative words in self-defeating dialogue include *should*, *always*, and *never*. This kind of talk tends to be absolute and makes little room for nuance, even though it masquerades as truth.

After pausing, I encourage them to ask themselves, "How long has this been going on? Is this the way I always talk to myself? Where did these ideas come from?" It's important to remember that we weren't born thinking of ourselves in critical and self-defeating ways, but over time, this kind of inner dialogue became a conditioned response that now lives outside of our conscious awareness. Typically, if we go far back enough, we start to recognize that the words we speak to ourselves are the words of one of our primary caregivers or another influential adult in our early years. When we say things like, "I'm not good enough," we think it's the truth. We conveniently forget that these sentiments have a totally different origin that is external to us. The voice might sound a lot like our own, but only because we've repeated it so much that it has become our own. Thankfully, we have a choice as to whether or not we will continue to recite these false statements to ourselves. We don't have to let them become the soundtrack in our heads as we go about our daily lives.

After answering those initial questions, I suggest that people also inquire: "Are my inner thoughts and beliefs saturated with self-criticism or with kindness, self-compassion, love, and encouragement? Which would I like to choose? How can I talk to myself as if I were my own best friend or beloved child?"

When we are figuring out ways to connect with self-love and self-care, aside from evaluating our inner dialogue, it's important to consider whether we have any energy drains that are holding us back. I've found that if we're not taking the time to care for ourselves (which can range from getting enough sleep to filling our lives with the people and activities we love), it's usually because we're busily pouring ourselves into others or being drained in some way.

You can refer back to Chapter 7 to identify any of the energy drains that might be sucking your attention away from caring for number one. If you're having difficulty, consider what your energy drains are, because this will help you to free up your bandwidth and to stop making excuses about not having enough "me" time.

In addition, energy drains can severely impact your sense of self-concept. If you're feeling low and not speaking very nicely to yourself, it might be difficult to determine whether that's because of an internal belief or because you're connected to someone who is making you feel that way. At the very least, it's a good idea to eliminate any external factors that may be contributing to a lack of self-love and self-care. It will be a lot easier to assess your situation accurately once you clear away the cobwebs.

Connecting with self-love and self-care is an ongoing journey that will require you to evaluate the contents of your life on a regular basis. What is it that may be depleting your energy? At the same time, what is it that gives you even more energy? The more you can remove or eliminate energy drains and move in the direction of things that revitalize your energy, the easier it will be to connect with a true sense of self-worth and self-confidence, as well as the parts of you that deserve more TLC and nurturing.

THE PRACTICES

#1: Keep a Self-Love Journal

Often, as we get caught in the fray of life, we can be overly hard on ourselves and forget all the things that make us lovable and worthy. This is why it's useful to keep an ongoing list of all your uniquely lovable qualities (the more specific, the better). Having a nighttime practice of both adding to the list and reading it to feel uplifted can be a powerful ongoing exercise in self-love.

I also advise getting help with this from friends, family, colleagues, and other trusted people in your life. Ask them, "What are your favorite things about me? What are three qualities you appreciate about me?" Again, specificity helps us to anchor the good feelings into our bodies, so something like, "I love the way your nose wrinkles when you laugh, and it's like you can't even contain the joy you feel," will have a stronger effect than, "You love to laugh."

Keep a section in your journal that's specifically for self-love. You can jot things down in the journal any time you think of them, but be sure to take a few minutes to read what you've written at bedtime. I especially enjoy doing this practice while looking in the mirror and speaking to myself in second person: "Oliver, I love and appreciate you for being a thoughtful dad, for putting your heart and soul into the healing work you do, for trusting your gut, etc."

Sometimes, it can also help to make this journal more visual and fill it with records of your "wins," including photos from graduation, your child's birth, a work milestone, an especially fun girls' night out, or anything that gave you a sense of wholeness and connection to yourself. Some of my clients and students have created self-love vision boards that remind them not just of their wonderful qualities, but also of the subtle and obvious ways they are supported and loved by the universe. This can be a wonderful counterpoint to the many negative thoughts we might tend to replay over and over in our heads during the day—and a beautiful way of patterning our subconscious with new, more high-vibration thoughts. Your self-love journal and vision board will be tangible reminders of how rich and abundant your life truly is.

#2: Enjoy the Silence

I highly recommend taking 10–15 minutes of solitude for this practice. Unplug from all your devices and take this time to be intentionally alone, still, and quiet. You might even wish to do this in a bathtub or when you're out in nature.

The purpose of this self-care practice is to learn to be with yourself and become accustomed to the deep inner silence that is an unchanging aspect of your true essence.

When we don't take the time to be with ourselves, with no particular goal in mind, the events of the day can often pile up until we are buried in them and completely exhausted. Solitude enables us to hit the reset button by allowing the flurry of activity to settle around us so that we are now the objective observer of our experience. We tap into that potent space of possibility that lives in the gap between our inhalation and exhalation. This is the peace that passes understanding, which many religious traditions have referred to, and that exists in moments of contemplation, prayer, and meditation.

Again, don't go into this with any goal in mind—not even meditation, which can cause the mind to react with rigidity. Instead, just offer yourself time to settle down and *be*, in the absence of external stimuli. Over time, you'll feel more peaceful, centered, and grounded—which is one of the greatest forms of self-care you can give yourself.

MORE RESOURCES AND FREE DOWNLOADS

Nurture yourself with self-love! Listen to the **Self-Love Meditation Audio** to deepen your relationship with yourself and cultivate self-compassion. Listen here:

https://dothisbeforebed.com/resource

CHAPTER 20

SLEEP

It's not very often that you see a chapter about sleep in a self-help book that's about energy! But, of course, you already know that the practices in this book are designed to be done at bedtime. Again, I want to reiterate that the reason I've selected bedtime is that I'm well aware of the benefits of shifting our energy in the hours preceding sleep.

Sleep is an incredibly important time that we too often take for granted. We spend a third of our lives asleep, but we don't frequently stop to think about the value of this time, and what's actually happening. As you already know, bedtime is when we can train the subconscious mind to shift our energy so that we are naturally moving into a higher vibration, which we will ideally remain in while we're sleeping. Indeed, accessing the full power of our sleep states is the missing key to our well-being—and through our conscious awareness in our waking state, we have the power to plant powerful seeds in our subconscious mind during our sleeping state (as well as the "in-between" times, which you'll shortly learn about!).

Let's explore this idea that sleep is a wonderful time during which to program the subconscious mind with new messages about the kind of life we would like to have. The subconscious mind is generally connected to our sleep states, because unlike the rest of our body, it continues to process information even while we're asleep. The subconscious mind is still pretty mysterious, but it's associated with the basal ganglia, also known as the "basement of the brain" and the axis on which the subconscious mind revolves. It's connected to a lot of our automatic behavior, such as our motor processes and deeper emotional responses. Many have surmised that the subconscious mind actually works best when we're in a sleeping state and the conscious mind, which has a lot of filters and patterns based on all the data we've acquired throughout our day, is essentially in off mode. Even though the conscious mind is powered off, the subconscious mind continues to work. It's busily powering involuntary functions like our breathing and heartbeat—and it's also in charge of the dreams that come through on any given night.

The science is still out with respect to how dreams actually occur, but in simple terms, we can view them as electrical signals in the brain that are pulling up images from the file drawer of the subconscious mind. Some dreams are a series of seemingly unrelated or nonsensical images and experiences, but others seem to convey a deeper message that some aspect of the subconscious wants to alert us to. Some scientists have even studied things like precognition (knowing the future before it happens), which can occur in dreams. Essentially, the subconscious mind is a treasure trove of unexplained possibilities that is especially mysterious when we get into the terrain of sleep.

The messages we send the subconscious in a hypnagogic state (the state between waking and sleeping) are the ones that tend to remain with us and to build new codes or patterns that the subconscious mind drinks in as if they were truth. And because confirmation bias is such a powerful aspect of our daily lives and reality, there's a way in which we will begin to magnetize experiences that align with the new, high-vibration emotional states that we're building through the practices in this book, which we're doing right before we go to sleep.

During the hypnagogic state, the brain gradually moves from the beta waves of our conscious waking state to the theta waves of our sleeping state. Let's talk a little bit about brain waves. Again, we're mostly in a high-frequency beta brain wave state when we're awake; the beta brain wave state can involve alertness, agitation, mental activity, and even activity in which we are attentive yet relaxed. This is the brain wave state that's associated with having our eyes open and being attuned to our surroundings, so that we can engage in problem-solving and decision-making. However, as we start to drift to sleep, we move into the alpha wave state. The alpha wave state is associated with meditation and tranquility, where we might be relaxed but not totally drowsy. From there, we gradually move into the theta brain wave state, which is a lower frequency and is connected to slower activity in the brain, including states of oneness and creativity. As we move into deep sleep, we enter the lowest brain wave state, which is delta. This is associated with a dreamless sleep—but even in this seemingly inactive state, the subconscious mind is very much still turned on.

Overall, all these brain wave states are important aspects of our process of healing and restoration. In addition, sleep can also be an extremely creative time during which we can experience not just restoration but the possibility of programming our brains with new energetic states.

Unfortunately, lots of people tend to have a variety of issues with sleep. Across the world, one in three people deal with insomnia. When our brains don't have the opportunity to move from beta to theta to delta states, our body doesn't have the opportunity to engage in its essential restorative functions, which are instrumental to our well-being.

Research has shown that sleep is connected to the processing of memories and a sense of hitting the reset button on our bodily functions (especially the ones frazzled by the day), but we don't really know if we sleep because we need to, or if we simply evolved to conduct these rejuvenating processes during sleep because it's just easier and more efficient than doing so when our bodies are awake. What some sleep scientists and energy healers have found is that it's actually possible to get great sleep in a very short amount of time rather than the requisite eight hours. Science is still trying to figure out how this is possible—but then again, science has always been somewhat in the dark when it comes to sleep.

Whatever the case, I know from firsthand experience that we can use our sleep not just to optimize the functions of our body but also to heal any limiting patterns we've been stuck in.

It's a great idea to look at some of the sleep patterns that we feel might be getting in the way of optimizing our "power off" time. However, there are some aspects of bedtime I'd like to reframe.

A common issue I find among students and clients is that they have a tendency to wake up between 3 and 5 A.M., which can feel disruptive and frustrating—especially if they're trying to optimize their sleep. However, what I've found is that the benefits of sleep during this time can also enter our waking hours! That's because 3 to 5 A.M. is the time during which the energy of the spirit realm is extremely active and the veil between our physical reality and the spirit realm is thin. We don't have any scientific proof of this yet, but many people, from poets to inventors, have noted that they are able to channel information that's integral to their work in this time frame.

If this is true for you, I suggest not attempting to drift back to sleep, but rather, taking advantage of this potent and literal "wake-up" call. If I find myself awake, I often pull up my phone and start writing down all the ideas that are likely to be racing through my head or to simply lie there and meditate. Sometimes, I wake up between 3 and 5 A.M. with a great deal of energy, almost as if I could run a marathon. This excess energy is not a bad thing, even though it might feel like it came out of left field! In fact, it's a wonderful time to wake up and smell the coffee, so to speak.

Other times, I've had students and clients wake up and notice what I call "angel numbers" (more about that in Chapter 21) on their clock or phone, like 3:33 or 4:44. I often associate repeating numbers with spiritual validation that somebody is on the right track, even though they may not know what the numbers mean in the moment. During these times, a seed is being planted that could be needed in a few days, a few weeks, or a month. It's a sign from the universe telling us that whatever we need will be there for us when we most require it. Again, from my experience, this generally tends to happen between 3 and 5 A.M., almost as if our spirit is attempting to communicate to us from across the veil. Don't forget to document this if it happens! When you look back, it will start to make sense.

Another aspect of sleep that can sometimes be troubling and that can get in the way of the capacity to really catalyze this time of restoration is something known as sleep paralysis. If you've ever experienced it, you know it occurs when you wake up and you can't move. It can be a frightening experience, but often, when this happens, it typically means that we're between two realms, the energetic and the physical, and we can't quite find our footing in either.

It's not a bad space to be in, although the effects on the body can be alarming. Instead of freaking out the next time this happens, you can consciously hold your breath for as long as possible. Basically, this forces you to come fully back into your body and to instantaneously ground yourself instead of remaining in that discombobulated limbo state.

Overall, there are so many incredible mystical states connected to sleep, and we can be grateful that we get to have this time—because it enables us not just to feel more well rested, but to also escape the burdens that we often experience in the physical world. Sleep can help us to recognize we have the capacity to be superpowered, waking up with greater energy and more inspiration, or opening ourselves up to traveling through the astral realm or even lucid dreaming so that we can bring answers from beyond the veil back into our daily lives. I've always felt that sleep is an incredible opportunity to bridge the gap between our physical reality and our spiritual reality. And once we learn to really tap into it and capture its gifts for our highest good, we discover that it holds a huge range of opportunities and adventures that are meant to expand our capacity and remind us of who we truly are!

THE PRACTICES

#1: Improve Your Sleep with Crystals

One thing a lot of successful and high-powered people also know is that the quantity of our sleep is not as important as the quality of our sleep. I personally love filling my living space with crystals, which are essential healing tools that help me to deepen my sleep and wake up refreshed, even if I'm only able to hit the hay for a few hours.

Their molecular structure often resonates with structures in our own physical and energetic bodies. Different crystals have different purposes, depending on their structure. Some of them can protect us through the absorption of negative energy, and others protect us by raising the vibration of the room. Most protect us simply by clearing any negativity that we've absorbed, which helps us to rest at ease.

I suggest using smoky quartz or black tourmaline, or other darker crystals for a greater sense of protection. I like to keep them in my bedroom to absorb negative energy, so that I don't unconsciously take any of it into my body and disrupt the flow of my energy as I sleep. However, it's important to periodically clear our crystals, especially when they've absorbed a lot of negative energy. You can do this by placing them in sunlight or moonlight, or burning sage and passing the smoke over your crystals.

I also love citrine, which is a powerful crystal that carries the energy of the sun. The sun is one of the most powerful sources for clearing energy and disinfects our energy body naturally. Citrine can mimic and duplicate the energy of the sun.

Another crystal I love is selenite. I place sticks or "wands" of selenite in each corner of the bedroom to form an energetic grid. This raises the vibration of the room and pulls down the energy of the angelic realms. When the angelic realm is present, negativity cannot get through.

You can do this exercise by placing all of the aforementioned crystals in your bedroom; I like to place smoky quartz, black tourmaline, and citrine on my nightstand or even under my pillow, and selenite at the four corners of the room. Ask your crystals to protect you from any negative energy and to raise the vibration of the room, so that you can sleep well and continue to have crystal-clear health. You'll definitely start feeling the effects that your crystals have on your sleep and on your life if you do this in the long term.

Don't forget to thank your crystals! Crystals positively interact with your body's energy field, and when they interact with high-vibration emotions like gratitude and love, this can amplify your sense of well-being. You can literally program your crystals with the energy of gratitude, acknowledging them for protecting you from negativity and keeping your energy clear and light so that you can truly absorb the restorative qualities of sleep, rather than allowing any lingering negative energy to impact these sacred hours.

#2: Learn to Astral Travel and Lucid Dream

Astral travel is based on the concept that our spirit, or consciousness, can detach from the physical body and travel through a realm of subtle energy that we don't always have immediate access to. Lucid dreaming is the capacity to achieve conscious awareness that you are dreaming, right in the midst of a dream. This practice will help you to do both.

Because our conscious mind is powered off during sleep, we can literally move through regions of the spirit world that may be connected to angelic beings or the energy bodies and souls of people we know, including those who are deceased.

However, not all of us consciously astral travel or lucid dream; often, our dreams are merely a messy regurgitation of the events of the day. While these kinds of dreams can also be valuable in helping us to sift through the symbols and experiences that have left their imprint on us, we can exercise greater agency when we move with more intention and curiosity through the astral landscape.

If you'd like to astral travel so that you can receive messages from a higher power while you sleep (and lucid dream so that you can actually recall them), this is a simple but powerful way to safely do so. The first step is to set your intention by calling on whatever you believe in—God, a higher power, the universe, angels, spirit guides, etc.—to protect your energy in your dream state and to guide you to higher planes within the astral realm. You might have a specific question you'd like an answer to, or you might just want to connect with that energy.

Next, engage in a simple breathing technique: Inhale for three counts, hold for three, exhale for three, and then hold for three. (This is similar to the four-count box breath, but three is a sacred number in many traditions, so I like using it for this particular process.) Do this as many times as you can. As you do this, state a simple affirmation, such as, "I am traveling to sacred realms in the astral plane in order to [fill in the blank with your intention], and I will remember everything I see and experience."

Soon, you'll find yourself going in and out of consciousness (this is known as the hypnagogic "in-between" state). Next, fill your entire body with a pure, powerful white light. At this point, pay attention to its source. Where does the light come from? If you can, let yourself follow this light as far as possible—beyond your city, state, country, etc. While you're doing this, don't hold on too tightly to wherever you are led. Let yourself drift off to sleep, and don't be surprised if you find yourself having vivid dreams about other realms. (Another variation of following the white light is to imagine the infinity sign spinning very rapidly and opening a portal that connects you to the astral realm.)

One student who did this exercise told me she was able to communicate with her deceased grandmother. It gave her a sense of hope and connection to the realms beyond the physical, as well as the awareness that our bonds of connection and love persist far beyond this lifetime.

MORE RESOURCES AND FREE DOWNLOADS

Optimize your sleep for deeper rest! Download the **Sleep Space Checklist** to help you create the perfect environment for restful, restorative sleep every night. Download here:

https://dothisbeforebed.com/resource

CHAPTER 21

SPIRITUALITY

When I think about spirituality, I think about the idea of spirit, which has so many different definitions in the realm of energy healing and the New Age. In my own terminology, spirit is a powerful guiding force. It is essentially energy that cannot be created or destroyed; nor can it be constrained by time, place, or language. It transcends all limited definitions, and yet, we instantly know it when we feel it.

Most of us have had an experience that is so permeated with awe and wonder that we know beyond a shadow of a doubt we've had an encounter with spirit—whatever we choose to call it. It is what enables us to recognize that there's something more vast than our narrow concepts of identity and reality. It is both magical and mundane. It is the energy, the life force, that powers consciousness and everything we are capable of perceiving.

It's apt that this is the final chapter of the book because if there's anything I hope to impart, it is that accessing the incredible power of spirit can offer us a greater sense of purpose, meaning, joy, and fulfillment.

The interesting thing is that, no matter what your religious beliefs or even your lack of beliefs might be, spirituality is something that often tends to be innately built into our ways of perceiving and engaging with reality. Even people with a rationalist, materialist perception of reality have had the experience of, say, being moved by a musical composition or the beauty of a sunset. Even if they don't call it "God" or "spirit," they're being imbued with that same experience of the mystery that transcends that which we "know" with our linear, rational minds.

Thankfully, the paradigms I teach are not meant to violate people's belief systems and ways of operating in the world, or to cause anyone to contort themselves into a worldview that just doesn't fit what they've been taught and have grown to accept. The amazing thing about spirituality is that it doesn't really matter what somebody's background, faith, or even lack of faith might be. The work I do is about helping people to experience a more visceral and tangible connection with their higher power in such a way that they have a direct line of communication with spirit that cannot be denied, because it just *is*, the same way gravity and the other laws of physics just are.

As I mentioned in the earlier chapters, there is nothing in particular you need to believe in order to have this experience of aligning with spirit. It's much more about being curious and open than it is about having preconceived answers about the mysteries of existence. It's enough to merely entertain the idea that we are so much more than a body—something that modern science is starting to corroborate—and that we have the capacity to expand our sense of possibility when we are connected to the energy realm.

This is why so many of the practices in this book are extremely potent—they're meant to strengthen our connection between physical and spiritual reality. The practices are also very helpful when it comes to updating our physical reality in such a way that we can experience an undiluted and direct connection to spirit. This is why I focus so much on clearing trauma and blocks that may be serving as obstacles to our communication with the divine.

There are many ways in which we can experience this powerful connection. For example, I know a lot of people who do it through prayer. My wife, Mandy, meditates in solitude. For me, my connection to spirit feels most palpable when I'm doing a healing or when I'm directly engaged in energy work. I have clients and students who experience spirit as a warm light coming down through the crown of their head and bathing their entire body in love. Other people I know experience it when they're deeply connected to nature.

Essentially, our unfiltered way of connecting with spirit, which is unique to each of us, enables us to experience a sense of purity and unconditional love that helps us get out of our heads and more deeply into our hearts. How do you feel that connection with the higher power? It's important to recognize your own access points and prioritize building them into your day in as intentional a way as possible.

Overall, the goal of spirituality is to help you to become more of who you are. It's not about having to do anything in particular, although our chosen access points can be extremely helpful. At the same time, the more we engage with spirit with our full conscious awareness, the more we will experience its presence throughout our daily lives. (In an ideal world, this would be the status quo—and with enough visionaries who are willing to move the needle of global consciousness, we can make it so!)

In the work I do with students and clients, I emphasize that spirit is our essential nature. When we attempt to answer the question, "Who am I?," as I outlined in Chapter 18, we come into closer contact with our true nature. We realize that the way we feel when we are simply being our truest, most authentic self is identical to how we feel when we connect with a higher power. We learn that whatever we've been seeking in the external world is within us. The further along we are on the spiritual path, the more we recognize that it's less about finding spirit "out there" in the world and more about looking within because spirit has been with us all along.

The fact that we hold everything we need inside of us at all times is something I always emphasize, especially because spirituality is often used as an escape. But the ironic thing is, connection with spirit helps us to connect with our humanity in an even deeper and more appreciative way. We often don't have to go very far in order to do this. When we deeply practice the tenets of our religious or spiritual belief system, we come to embody spirit. We inevitably come to the conclusion that whatever we've been searching for on the outside is actually on the inside. All roads lead to Rome. We don't get to this realization through intellectualizing, though. We simply have to do the work to land here.

The "work" often begins with a few simple steps. All of the practices in this book are meant to help you hone your relationship with spirit, and one of the things I specifically like to suggest to students and clients is that they practice building their muscle for living in divine synchronicity.

Synchronicity, which occurs when a series of seemingly unrelated events start to form a meaningful picture in one's personal reality, has transformed my life. I used to want to control everything with my mind. But at some point, I learned that we're bombarded with up to 40,000 bits of information per second, in the form of things we might see or experience during the day. Because it's so much information, our conscious mind grasps very little of it. That means we're missing out on about 99.99 percent of the things we're exposed to. This is why attempting to live through the conscious mind alone is an incomplete way of doing life. It's much better to be guided by divine synchronicity.

I constantly ask to be guided because I understand that a higher power knows and sees everything and can take me to the places I need to go in order to be connected to spirit at all times. I have often experienced divine synchronicity when my initial plans don't work out—instead, a thought or inspiration seems to come out of nowhere and propels me in the right direction in ways I hadn't anticipated (and certainly, in ways my mind couldn't orchestrate).

For example, I once prayed for a sign about a business-related issue I was having some challenges with. As I was driving on the highway, a truck passed in front of me with a sign that said: "Danger: Radioactive! Don't get too close!" I immediately noticed that the big sign I had asked for was right in front of my nose, only a minute after making that request to the universe. Looking back, although it was not the sign I wanted to receive, I surrendered to it and later realized that I'd definitely dodged a bullet.

From my experience, many of us need a series of signs before we're able to trust our intuition. But if we get into the habit of listening to what the universe is telling us in the moment, it becomes easier to read the signs, and it completely changes the game.

Another aspect of living in divine synchronicity and watching out for communications from spirit can be found in the realm of angel numbers. In numerology, angel numbers refer to numeric sequences, usually three or four numbers long, that repeat. Examples include 1111 or 4444. If you're thinking about something like a big decision you're about to make that you might be unsure about, seeing an angel number provides validation that you're moving in the right direction. This is similar to seeing animals like eagles or hawks, which can also be an affirmative sign from our higher power. Other meaningful synchronicities include hearing a song with a message that resonates with us perfectly in the moment.

Of course, the opposite is also true. We might receive negative signs *not* to move in a particular direction. Such signs might include seeing broken glass, stubbing a toe, or encountering anything that opens up Pandora's box of negativity—like bumper-to-bumper traffic, a stranger being rude to you, missing all the green lights when you're already late, etc. When these occur, I usually recognize them as signs that my spirit guides are attempting to communicate with me and steward me in a better direction.

Whatever the case, we are always being guided by spirit, and we can attune to this in a more intentional way at every moment. We are never alone, and there is something in and beyond us that is striving to remind us of that fact. But we *do* need to practice paying attention to how signs from the divine show up. Again, using the practices in this book will be instrumental in helping you open up the channel of communication. The more open you are to spirit, the more your gifts will be activated in the world.

Often, suffering comes from an inability to access the gifts of spirit that each of us is born with. But when we are able to connect in a deep, immediate, and powerful way, which is often as simple as getting out of our own way and surrendering to the true nature of the universe (hint: it's love and interconnectedness!), something within us gets activated. Life transforms for the better. We recognize that we are not here to struggle and suffer. We are here to be in a state of flow, and to recognize that our human side and our spirit side are meant to work together in synergistic harmony.

THE PRACTICES

#1: Connect with Your Higher Power

This is a simple practice you can use anytime, especially when you feel lost or disconnected from the light that lives within you. Place your hand on your heart. Say the affirmation: "I am now open to receive guidance from a higher power: guidance that will speed up whatever it is that's in the highest good for me to experience; guidance that will help me avoid any unnecessary pain and suffering. Thank you." Let this affirmation put you at ease. Know that you're being divinely guided to exactly where you need to be at the right time, without any unnecessary stress. Do this for seven days and notice how much lighter and more present you feel.

#2: Call in Divine Light

Take a deep breath and release a long exhale. Imagine a pure, divine white light coming down from the sky, down from the heavens, filling your entire body up so that it fully envelops you. This is the light of unconditional love, of the divine presence that is always around us, whether we feel it or not. Inside this warm white light, say, "I call upon all the angels and archangels of pure light and love. I am safe. I am protected. I am loved. I am connected to the divine at all times." Inhale once more. As you do, imagine that this bubble of white light is becoming even stronger and brighter all around you, until it is the one reality that touches everything in your life. As you exhale, release any and all stagnant, negative energy. As you do this, know that you are protected. Know that you are loved. Feel that everything in your life—your work, relationships, and all that you love—is being touched by this light. Feel the light emanating from your heart out into the world. In this state, notice if there are any divine messages that might be coming through in the form of thoughts, ideas, images, or emotions.

MORE RESOURCES AND FREE DOWNLOADS

Deepen your spiritual connection! Listen to the **Spiritual Awakening Meditation Audio** to help you connect with your higher self and the divine as you drift into sleep. Liste here:

https://dothisbeforebed.com/resource

CONCLUSION

We've come to the end of this particular journey, but in truth, it's just the beginning.

While the practices in this book are meant to be utilized in the evening, they can be brought to bear at any moment in your life, for any situation you're going through. Overall, the purpose of *Do This Before Bed* is to give you quick, easy tools that you can use whenever you need them in order to connect with your higher self, that aspect of you that is not limited by the three-dimensional world but that simultaneously exists in the realm of energy.

Remember, your imagination is one of your superpowers. Anything that has ever been invented once started out as a seed in somebody's imagination—and then, with the power of intention and mindset, it was birthed into the world of form. My hope is that in reading this book, you will be able to tap into the power of your imagination to express and realize more and more of your infinite self. From here, you'll manifest beautiful things beyond what you ever believed possible.

I want to offer my encouragement and full belief that you can absolutely have the life of your dreams, even if it has not felt within reach in the past. It's not a matter of overhauling everything in your day-to-day. It begins with becoming more receptive to new possibilities and inviting in a little bit of magic, even if you're somewhat skeptical. However, I encourage you to mix it up in any way you feel best serves you. Incorporate the four foundational practices into your bedtime routine, and also connect with the other tools, depending on what it is you need and are longing for in your life at any given moment.

While I have seen the tools in this book improve the lives of countless people by helping them to increase their sense of clarity, peace, and connection to their authentic truth, please know that *you* are your own best authority. Don't do anything that creates a sense of conflict with your soul. In fact, when people in your life insist, "Hey, this is something that you absolutely have to do," it doesn't matter who that person is—if it doesn't feel right, ignore their advice and follow your gut. Although I've intentionally written this book to address a number of issues and offer you a slew of techniques that I have seen work wonders in the lives of millions of people, none of this is meant to be a one-size-fits-all.

No matter what, allow the techniques in this book to spark your creativity. We're all wired to be creative, and one of the best ways to get out of internal conflict and into a sense of alignment is to tune in to what your creativity is moving you toward. You can also use your heart to ask yourself, "Does this sit right with me? Does it feel good, or does it feel heavy? Does it feel like I'm in conflict, or like I'm in alignment?" Finding the answers to these questions will offer you ultimate freedom. Because at the end of the day, this book is about teaching you to follow your own compass as you surf the waters of the energetic realms.

Overall, I believe that if you're reading this book right now, it's because you are primed to be the best version of yourself. Often, this is a joyous process, but please be gentle with yourself if you feel overwhelmed by the changes you're experiencing. Change might feel overwhelming, but the person you were in the past doesn't even exist anymore, and they won't get you to where you want to go. What you are stepping into is completely different. Because, as you release all the aspects of your life that are not yet healed, which is what the tools in this book will help you to do, better things will become available. New possibilities will open up. Your preferences will most likely evolve. Embrace the countless opportunities that open up and lead you to your future self.

You've already made a huge leap by reading this book, so don't worry about where you're going to land, wherever you're going. Many of my students and clients will tell you: It's a place that is exactly the one you've been waiting for. And if the changes you want to make haven't happened yet, enjoy the ride. Relax, have fun, and focus on something else. Beautiful things are coming your way, and there's no need to put yourself through the stress of worrying about it. And just know, even in the times when you might not feel it, you are extremely supported and guided by many benevolent forces, seen and unseen.

Also, always remember that you are not your thoughts. You are not your emotions. You are not your physical body. You are not what has happened to you in the past. You are not your pain or your trauma. You are pure energy, pure love, pure light. You are here to learn valuable soul lessons. My hope is that your particular lessons can be learned with greater ease, joy, curiosity, and awareness, so that all of it feels like an unfolding adventure.

With that, I encourage you to keep doing these practices at bedtime. Soon enough, you will realize that you're not just dreaming about the life you've always wanted. You're living it in every waking moment.

Love,
Oliver

ABOUT THE AUTHOR

OLIVER NIÑO is an entrepreneur, energy healer, author, and spiritual activation expert. He is the creator of Geo Love Healing, an online company designed to help individuals master their energy, unblock themselves, and become healers. Oliver has performed more than 30,000 healing sessions and has trained people from more than 60 countries in his energy healing methodology. In testimonials, his clients state that they have progressed more from just one healing session or from his 30-day program than from decades of therapy and personal development. A highly esteemed energy healing expert, Oliver and his brand have amassed a loyal global following, including many celebrity clients.

www.spiritualactivator.com

NOTES

NOTES

NOTES

NOTES

NOTES

NOTES

Hay House Titles of Related Interest

YOU CAN HEAL YOUR LIFE, the movie,
starring Louise Hay & Friends
(available as an online streaming video)
www.hayhouse.com/louise-movie

THE SHIFT, the movie,
starring Dr. Wayne W. Dyer
(available as an online streaming video)
www.hayhouse.com/the-shift-movie

***

DIVINE MASTERS, ANCIENT WISDOM: Activations to Connect with Universal Spiritual Guides, by Kyle Gray

THE LIFE OF YOGANANDA: The Story of the Yogi Who Became the First Modern Guru, by Philip Goldberg

POWER VS. FORCE: The Hidden Determinants of Human Behavior, by Dr. David R. Hawkins

YOGA, POWER & SPIRIT: Patanjali the Shaman, by Alberto Villoldo, Ph.D.

YOU ARE MORE THAN YOU THINK YOU ARE: Practical Enlightenment for Everyday Life, by Kimberly Snyder

All of the above are available at your local bookstore,
or may be ordered by contacting Hay House (see next page).

***

We hope you enjoyed this Hay House book. If you'd like to receive our online catalog featuring additional information on Hay House books and products, or if you'd like to find out more about the Hay Foundation, please contact:

Hay House LLC, P.O. Box 5100, Carlsbad, CA 92018-5100
(760) 431-7695 or (800) 654-5126
www.hayhouse.com® • www.hayfoundation.org

———

Published in Australia by:
Hay House Australia Publishing Pty Ltd
18/36 Ralph St., Alexandria NSW 2015
Phone: +61 (02) 9669 4299
www.hayhouse.com.au

Published in the United Kingdom by:
Hay House UK Ltd
1st Floor, Crawford Corner,
91–93 Baker Street, London W1U 6QQ
Phone: +44 (0)20 3927 7290
www.hayhouse.co.uk

Published in India by:
Hay House Publishers (India) Pvt Ltd
Muskaan Complex, Plot No. 3,
B-2, Vasant Kunj, New Delhi 110 070
Phone: +91 11 41761620
www.hayhouse.co.in

———

Let Your Soul Grow

Experience life-changing transformation—one video at a time—with guidance from the world's leading experts.

www.healyourlifeplus.com

OLIVER NIÑO is an entrepreneur, energy healer, author, and spiritual activation expert. He is the creator of Geo Love Healing, an online company designed to help individuals master their energy, unblock themselves, and become healers. Oliver has performed more than 30,000 healing sessions and has trained people from more than 60 countries in his energy healing methodology. In testimonials, his clients state that they have progressed more from just one healing session or from his 30-day program than from decades of therapy and personal development. A highly esteemed energy healing expert, Oliver and his brand have amassed a loyal global following, including many celebrity clients.

www.spiritualactivator.com

Hay House USA
P.O. Box 5100, Carlsbad, CA 92018-5100
(760) 431-7695 or (800) 654-5126
www.hayhouse.com®

Front cover design: 99 Designs
Case design: Karim J. Garcia
Photo of Oliver Niño: Hannah Rose Gray

Printed in the United States of America